EVERY DAY IS A FAITH DAY

A Practical Guide to Steadfast Faith

by

Philip Steele

Little Rock
2020

Unless otherwise noted, all scripture is from the King James Version of the Bible.

Scripture quotations marked AMPC are from The Amplified Bible, Old Testament ©1965,1987 by the Zondervan Corporation. The Amplified New Testament© 1958,1987 by The Lockman Foundation.

Scripture quotations marked (NEB) are taken from the NEW ENGLISH BIBLE, Copyright© 1961, 1970 by Cambridge University Press, Oxford University Press. All rights reserved.

Scripture quotations marked (Wuest) are taken from The New Testament: An Expanded Translation by Kenneth S. Wuest, copyright © 1961 William B. Eerdmans Publishing Co., Grand Rapids, Michigan.

Scripture quotations marked (YLT) are taken from the 1898 YOUNG'S LITERAL TRANSLATION OF THE HOLY BIBLE by J.N. Young, (Author of the Young's Analytical Concordance), public domain.

Every Day Is a Faith Day: A Practical Guide to Steadfast Faith

Copyright © 2020 by Philip Steele

Published by Faith 2 Fe Publishing,
P.O. Box 242692, Little Rock, AR

www.publishyourfaith.com

ISBN-13: 978-1-949934-38-0

Printed in the United States of America. All rights reserved under International Copyright Law. No part of this publication may be reproduced, stored in a retrieval system, or transmitted in any other form (i.e., electronic, mechanical, photocopy, recording or any other means), except for brief quotations in printed reviews, without the prior written permission of the author.

DEDICATION

May this book bring glory to God and to the Lord Jesus Christ. I am forever grateful to have been chosen to carry this revelation of faith and the power of His Word.

CONTENTS

1. THE HOW-TO'S OF FAITH 1

2. FAITH IS A "STANDING ON" 15

3. UNCHANGEABLE.. 27

4. SUBSTANCE AND EVIDENCE 37

5. GOD'S FAITH WON'T FAIL.................................. 49

6. A BALANCE IN BELIEVING 57

7. THE DEVELOPMENT OF FAITH........................... 67

8. RETAIN THE WORD THAT WAS HEARD 81

9. ADDING SELF-CONTROL AND PATIENCE 87

10. ADDING THE FORCE OF LOVE 111

11. DAILY FAITH FOR DAILY VICTORY................. 125

FOREWORD

Several years ago, I was told by a pastor friend of mine that when we get to heaven, faith will no longer be required, "...after all, we're in heaven; what could we possibly need faith for?"

Nothing could be further from the truth. Faith is not a commodity that is traded, or outdated. It is a way of life. The Scripture tells us that the just shall live by faith.

Faith pleases God. Without it, you can't please Him. *"When the Son of man cometh, shall He find faith on the earth?"* (Luke 18:8).

Every day is a faith day. Every day is an opportunity to use your faith. Someone said faith is like a muscle; if you don't use it, you lose it. You should give your faith an assignment every day. It pleases God, and it keeps your faith active.

What's your faith working on today?

Pastor Happy Caldwell

Happy Caldwell Ministries

PO Box 26207

Little Rock, Arkansas 72221

INTRODUCTION

Over twenty years ago, my wife Michelle and I hosted a home Bible study, and a lady who attended our bible study gave me a tape series by Kenneth Copeland entitled *"Establishing Your Heart on the Word of God."* The series was recorded at a London Victory Campaign, and on each tape, Brother Copeland taught from the 112th Psalm about how to establish your heart on the Word of God.

I was supernaturally drawn to this series. At the time, it seemed as though I was spiritually dehydrated, and this series was the water for which I had been thirsting. There was something different about those messages. Each one spoke directly to my spirit. However, what I did not realize at that moment in time was that I was hearing the spirit of faith. It was the spirit of faith that caused those messages to come alive and minister to me supernaturally.

Later, my wife and I received a tape series by Charles Capps entitled *"Faith: The Law of the New Covenant."* As I listened to those tapes, I learned that faith is a spiritual law, and there are principles that make that law work. I discovered that one of my biggest problems was one inch

EVERY DAY IS A FAITH DAY

below my nose... my mouth! I learned that I could have what I say, and that whatever I say, good or bad, is going to come to me in abundance.

As I applied the principles, my life began to change, and I began to see victory after victory. The principles of establishing my heart on the Word carried my wife and me through to victory when we faced a life-threatening challenge in connection with the birth of our daughter, Angela. Over the years, God has built principles of victory and faith into our hearts, and our lives are an example of His Word at work.

One evening, the Lord said to me, "Turn to Hebrews 11:3." I turned to this verse and read the following: *"Through faith we understand that the worlds were framed by the word of God, so that things which are seen were not made of things which do appear."*

The Lord instructed me, "Build people's faith and frame their world by My Word."

I responded, "Lord, how can I build people's faith? I do not even have enough money to get around the block." The Lord began to show me how to live by faith, how to operate my faith, and to frame my world by the Word of God. We have been living that way ever since that day.

Recently, the Lord said to me, "Every day is a faith day!" I realized there is not a day when faith is unnecessary. We use our faith every day.

In this book, you will find the lessons I have learned concerning faith from my study of the Word and from the great men and women of faith who God has brought into

INTRODUCTION

our lives. You can take these truths and apply them to your life so that you, too, can make "Every day a faith day!"

Philip Steele

CHAPTER ONE

The How-to's of Faith

THERE ARE MANY "DO-IT-YOURSELF" shows on television today. You can even search YouTube for videos on how to make specific recipes, how to play the guitar, or how to change a transmission. I appreciate the fact that we can access the instruction we need to achieve so many different tasks.

My goal in this book is to provide you with simple instructions. I want you to be able to apply your faith in any given area you encounter to achieve the success that God has planned for you.

These instructions will explain the basic fundamentals of faith, as well as help guide you to examine any area of your life where you are experiencing difficulties in applying your faith.

EVERY DAY IS A FAITH DAY

Faith is the lifestyle of the believer. If you want God's results of peace, joy, success, etc., you will need to employ faith daily. If it is accessed daily, it must be maintained daily. Every day is a faith day.

By Faith

ROMANS 1:17
17 For therein is the righteousness of God revealed from faith to faith: as it is written, The just shall live by faith.

***

2 CORINTHIANS 5:7
7 For we walk by faith, not by sight.

In these two verses, we see the phrase *"by faith."* We walk by faith, and we live by faith. That little, two-letter word *by* is a preposition that denotes "the channel or the means by which something is done."

The Scripture declares twice that we live and walk by faith. *The New Testament: An Expanded Translation* by Kenneth Wuest provides the following version of 2 Corinthians 5:7, *"...through faith, we order our manner of life..."*

The way we are to live and conduct our lives is by or through the means of faith. In Chapter 11 of Hebrews, the phrase *"by faith"* is used 16 times. In the same chapter, the phrase *"through faith"* is used five times.

Every time the phrase *"by faith"* or *"through faith"* is used in this chapter, it describes something that was done

2

THE HOW TO'S OF FAITH

by that person. It is telling us that these things were done by faith.

HEBREWS 11:8
8 By faith Abraham, when he was called to go out into a place which he should after receive for an inheritance, obeyed; and he went out, not knowing whither he went.

***

HEBREWS 11:11
11 Through faith also Sara herself received strength to conceive seed, and was delivered of a child when she was past age, because she judged him faithful who had promised.

***

HEBREWS 11:24
24 By faith Moses, when he was come to years, refused to be called the son of Pharaoh's daughter." He forsook Pharaoh's house.

The Word states that they accomplished all these things by faith. Often, we will read those passages and say, "Oh, yes! Amen. They did all those things by faith." The question to ask yourself is this: How do I do something by faith?

You may say, "I remodeled this myself." Then, the question is asked, "How did you do it?" You can tell me you did it yourself, but can you tell me how you did it?

It is easy to say, "Well, you've just got to have faith. You've got to believe." But how do you do it?

3

EVERY DAY IS A FAITH DAY

How do I walk something out from beginning to end by faith? How do I get from Point A to Point B by faith? Just telling people, "You have to do it by faith," doesn't tell them much.

How did Abraham believe God? He did it by faith. Exactly *how* did he do it by faith? I am repeating this thought for a reason. People may tell you, "We have to live by faith." But they don't tell you *how* to live by faith.

Every person who has done anything by faith first learned to do it through hearing the Word of God preached. How do we know this? Because that is how faith comes.

ROMANS 10:17

17 So then faith cometh by hearing, and hearing by the word of God.

The first step in achieving anything by faith is to understand the origin of faith. Faith comes by hearing the Word of God. God's Word is the source of faith or the wellspring of faith.

I enjoy drinking Perrier® water. You can read on the label, "bottled at the source." Then, it tells you where the spring is located.

The Word of God is the spring, the source of faith. Your faith can be strengthened by what I say. A certain amount of faith will come from hearing the minister preach or share a testimony, but, ultimately, the source of faith is the Word of God. When you see, hear, and declare what the Word says, it provides a gushing fountain of faith to nurture your life.

Never forget it is the Word of God that produces faith!

4

THE HOW TO'S OF FAITH

Steps of Faith Require a Clear Image

The Word of God produces a faith that can look past the seen and see the unseen. Many times, people try to take steps of faith without having a clear image. That clear image can only be produced by God's Word.

2 CORINTHIANS 4:18
18 While we look not at the things which are seen, but at the things which are not seen: for the things which are seen are temporal; but the things which are not seen are eternal.

Paul starts off by saying, *"While we look not at the things which are seen."* We must become more accustomed to living, acting, and walking by faith than we are accustomed to living, acting, and walking by our natural eyesight. The things which can be seen with our natural physical eyes are in the natural arena, and they are a reality. But Paul also says there are things that are not seen with the natural, physical eyes.

We are instructed to look at the things which are not seen. It is possible! We can look past what is seen and focus on what is not seen. Faith is the method to achieve this.

When you spend time meditating on the Word of God, you will begin to see things by faith. And as you continue meditating on the Word, the faith image will gradually develop until you can see a clear, sharp image of the thing for which you hope or desire. Eventually, the image built by the Word will be clearer than the natural image.

5

EVERY DAY IS A FAITH DAY

One pilot was training to be instrument rated.[1] His instructor told him that flying by instruments will make more sense than flying by what you can physically see.

In the aircraft, the radar is accessing details that the pilot cannot access by looking out the window. An instrument-rated pilot can navigate his way through a storm system by following the radar. The pilot may be in whiteout conditions, and the horizon may not be visible. Even though the pilot's physical eyes are not able to see clearly, he is trained to fly according to what the radar is indicating.

I was flying to Texas recently. I looked out the window and saw we were in a cloud. It didn't even seem to me like we were moving because I couldn't see anything. After the flight, the pilot admitted, "Yes, that feels different. You have to train yourself to fly by what the instruments tell you and not by what you can see."

When we walk by faith, we face the same challenge. How do you walk by faith and not by sight? How do you fly an aircraft by the instruments instead of by what you see?

You must train yourself to have confidence in what the instrument of faith indicates. You must become more comfortable with the report of faith than the information coming into your five physical senses.

---

1 This refers to qualifications pilots must have to fly under Instrument Flight Rules.

6

THE HOW TO'S OF FAITH

Faith Sees What the Word of God Says

ROMANS 4:17-21

17 (As it is written, I have made thee a father of many nations,) before him whom he believed, even God, who quickeneth the dead, and calleth those things which be not as though they were.

18 Who against hope believed in hope, that he might become the father of many nations, according to that which was spoken, So shall thy seed be.

19 And being not weak in faith, he considered not his own body now dead, when he was about an hundred years old, neither yet the deadness of Sarah's womb:

20 He staggered not at the promise of God through unbelief; but was strong in faith, giving glory to God;

21 And being fully persuaded that, what he had promised, he was able also to perform.

The end result of faith caused Abraham to become the father of many nations. He didn't live in line with the information that his physical body supplied. Abraham allowed what was spoken to be the radar by which he conducted his life. As such, he conducted his life according to that portion of verse 18, which says, *"...according to that which was spoken, So shall thy seed be."*

Hope has the power to develop a different picture inside of our hearts. In the natural, the picture Abraham saw was a 100-year-old body and a 90-year-old, barren wife. Sarah had always been incapable of having a child. Now,

7

EVERY DAY IS A FAITH DAY

both of them were well past the age of producing children. That was the natural picture available to Abraham.

He had to obtain a different image from the words that had been spoken by God. Faith comes by hearing what the Word says! Abraham decided to allow what God said to have greater influence than what he could see. Abraham started "flying by the instruments" instead of by what he could see.

In verse 19, the Bible says, *"And being not weak in faith, he considered not his own body..."* We get the idea that Abraham was fully aware of his physical condition. He knew how old he was. He knew the challenges he was facing. However, in walking by faith, he did not consider his advanced age to be a reason that would prevent God's promise from coming to pass.

Verse 20 says, *"He staggered not at the promise of God through unbelief; but was strong in faith, giving glory to God."* What God had spoken became bigger than what Abraham could see.

When you are walking by faith, what God says becomes more influential than all of the information coming through your physical senses. It will get to the point where you believe there is no possible way it *can't* happen. That is when you are past having any doubt.

How did Abraham reach the place where he did not consider his body to be a reason that God's promise could not take place? Verse 18 says, *"Who against hope [natural human hope] [he] believed in hope [hope produced by the Word of God]..."*

THE HOW TO'S OF FAITH

The word *hope* can be defined as an expectation of evil or an expectation of good. In the natural, there was a constant expectation or dread that nothing was going to change. Dread came against the image God had given.

It was this second hope, the expectation of good, that Abraham chose to consider, and it produced an expectation of good. Abraham saw an image of himself as the father of a multitude. He envisioned fruitfulness, children, and life. God's image contrasted with the image of barrenness, impotence, and impossibility.

Abraham gave his attention to the image God was giving him. If Abraham had chosen to focus on the other image, he would have never seen the promise of God come to pass. He would have never become the father of many nations.

Faith Focuses on the Unseen

This is what God said; this is how it will be. This is what God declared; this is the way it will occur. Walking and living by faith is more than just knowing the principles or the formulas of faith. You won't be successful just because you know how it is *supposed* to work. You must know how to work it. Abraham learned how to do this by faith.

For example, a person may be battling symptoms of the flu, and their coworker may ask, "Are you sick?"

That person may respond by saying, "No! Bless God, I am not sick. I feel great." But, in reality, the person does not feel great. Denying the reality of how they really feel

9

is not walking by faith. Many people fail in their faith walk because they have a formula for faith that does not have its basis in the Word of God.

Seeing by faith requires focusing on the unseen. That doesn't mean you deny what is seen. Instead, it means that what is seen doesn't have your focus. You are healed by faith. Just because you don't feel well, does not mean you are not healed. You can stand against the illness while it is raging in your body because you see something different by faith.

We do not look at what is evident or what is felt. Instead, we look, by faith, at what is not seen. What was evident in Abraham's case? It was the fact that he was physically past the age to father a child. But what did Abraham do? He looked past that picture of what was evident or seen (his advanced age), and he looked at or focused his attention on the unseen, which was God's promise that he would father a child.

The promise developed such a clear image in Abraham that his condition changed. Abraham's outward appearance didn't change, but how he saw his body changed. He began to see it through faith.

HEBREWS 11:3
3 Through faith we understand that the worlds were framed by the word of God, so that things which are seen were not made of things which do appear.

The New Testament: An Expanded Translation by Kenneth Wuest says, *"...by means of faith we perceive that the natural universe and the God-appointed ages of time*

THE HOW TO'S OF FAITH

were equipped and fitted by God's word for the purpose for which they were intended. And it follows therefore, that that which we see did not come into being out of that which is visible."

The material universe, what can be seen, felt, touched, and handled, did not come into being out of that which is visible to the natural physical eye. Everything we see in this universe did not originate from what is visible. What I need does not depend on what is visible. It is accessed by faith! This is how we access our supply.

By faith, we can perceive that the universe was framed or fitted for its intended purpose by the Word of God. We perceive and understand this by faith that is derived from God's Word.

The Word of God will bring into my life what is needed to frame and fit my life for its intended purpose. As such, the Word of God will provide all of my personal needs (health, financial, etc.) through the channel of my faith.

It doesn't matter whether we can see with our physical eyes. What matters, and what will produce a change in our lives, is staying focused on what God said. Then, change can begin to occur.

If you talk to people long enough, you will begin to understand what they are seeing and what they perceive. What that person is saying is what that person is seeing. That is what they believe.

When your friend says, "I don't see how we are going to make it," that is what they are seeing. They don't *see* how

EVERY DAY IS A FAITH DAY

they are going to make it. They are looking at the wrong picture. They are looking at what is seen.

They may look at their checkbook and say, "We are not going to make it," because of what they are seeing. They begin to plan what they can do or not do based on what they see. Now, they are living by the bank balance instead of by faith.

You can have the same circumstances, yet when you look at your checkbook, you take the Word of God and call for abundance. You start calling for more than enough and begin to declare what the Word of God says. "Father, I thank You that my checking account, my savings account, my investment accounts are full to the overflow. There is more than enough. We have all and abound unto every good work."

You may have the same checking balance as the other person, but you are seeing something the other person doesn't see. You are ordering your life by what the Word of God says; you are walking by faith and not by sight (2 Cor. 5:7).

The first thing that changed in Abraham was not his body, his strength, or his ability to have a child. The first thing that changed was how he saw himself. Abraham saw himself as being able to have a child. He saw Sarah as being able to bear a child. Then, the change occurred.

First, you have to see it. When you begin to see it, the ability, the strength, the financial victory begins to manifest in your life. You will get to the point where there is no possible way that you can see yourself failing. You

THE HOW TO'S OF FAITH

can only see yourself succeeding because you are seeing it the way God said it.

I remember when I began to operate these principles in my life. I was working for a division of a major insurance company that provided billing for doctors' offices throughout the Kansas City area. I went to work one morning feeling very ill. My head was swimming, and my body ached. I've never been one to give in to illness, so I got on the bus and went to work. But I was sick! Finally, the manager came to me and said, "You just need to go home! You are not going to be productive, and you don't want to give it to everyone else."

I said, "Okay" and took the bus home. I knew I had a choice to make. I could sit there and suffer or work the Word. I flipped over to Isaiah 53:5 where it says, "But he was wounded for our transgressions, he was bruised for our iniquities: the chastisement of our peace was upon him; and with his stripes we are healed." I declared that verse out loud and said, "I choose to believe that I am healed." I knew it was up to me. Faith came alive in me! The symptoms began to leave my body. By the time Michelle came home that evening, I had no symptoms at all.

I had been progressively building my faith in these things. It didn't just happen because I picked up the Word and confessed Isaiah 53:5. It happened because I had been steadily building an image inside myself over a period of weeks and months that I am healed of the Lord.

13

EVERY DAY IS A FAITH DAY

Eventually, that Scripture created an image of healing that became so vivid and so clear to me, even though everything in my body said, "You are not healed. You are not well." When I said, "I choose to believe I am healed. I am well in Jesus' name," it had to leave because I no longer saw myself as being sick. That's how it will work every time.

I can say "every time" because that is one of the "how to's" of faith. If you don't begin to change what you are seeing, if you don't see what God said instead of what you see in the natural realm, you will struggle. When you are faced with a situation, go to the Word of God and declare, "This is what the Word says." Meditate on what the Word says. "Lord, Your Word says this about the situation. Thank You that this is what I have."

Stay focused on what the natural eye cannot see, on what God said. He said the phrase "by faith" 16 times in Chapter 11 of Hebrews. By faith, the victory will come. By faith, healing will manifest. By faith, the financial issue will be resolved. By faith, that child will be saved. By faith, a marriage will be strengthened. By faith, everything you need will come into your life to do everything God wants you to do.

CHAPTER TWO

Faith Is a "Standing On"

THE LORD SPOKE THESE WORDS to me recently: "Preach faith, teach faith, and live by faith. The victory follows the teaching of faith. Faith is the focus: Faith in My Word, faith in Me, and faith in My ability."

1 JOHN 5:4

4 For whatsoever is born of God overcometh the world: and this is the victory that overcometh the world, even our faith.

The enemy has attacked the teaching of faith because it is the method of victory over the world. It is the message of triumph. The victory follows the teaching of faith.

1 TIMOTHY 4:1

1 Now the Spirit speaketh expressly, that in the latter times some shall depart from the faith, giving heed to seducing spirits, and doctrines of devils;

EVERY DAY IS A FAITH DAY

ROMANS 1:17

17 For therein is the righteousness of God revealed from faith to faith: as it is written, The just shall live by faith.

***

ROMANS 1:17 AMPC

17 For in the Gospel a righteousness which God ascribes is revealed, both springing from faith and leading to faith [disclosed through the way of faith that arouses to more faith]. As it is written, The man who through faith is just and upright shall live and shall live by faith.

If we are justified by faith, we have to live by faith to continue in that position of righteousness. If I don't continue to live by faith, advancing from faith to faith, I will have a setback that will begin to affect my sense of righteousness and justification.

2 CORINTHIANS 5:7

7 For we walk by faith, not by sight.

We are instructed to live by faith and to walk by faith. But how do we accomplish this task?

2 CORINTHIANS 5:7 AMPC

7 For we walk by faith [we regulate our lives and conduct ourselves by our conviction or belief respecting man's relationship to God and divine things, with trust and holy fervor; thus we walk] not by sight or appearance.

A regulation is a code or a system by which we function. As believers, we regulate our lives by faith. We operate our day to day lives by faith and not by sight or appearance.

Many make the mistake of thinking that as long as they are not paying attention to what they physically see,

FAITH IS A "STANDING ON"

they are in faith. That is not true! They might be in denial, mental assent, or lacking knowledge. Being in faith is not ignoring the situation.

If I am exercising my faith for an increase in finances, I may have to work overtime, pick up extra shifts or look for some side jobs. Walking by faith requires me to regulate my life by what I believe and add the natural effort to what I believe in my heart.

> **HEBREWS 11:1**
> **1 Now faith is the substance of things hoped for, the evidence of things not seen.**

If we do not know what faith is, we will not know when the substance or evidence of faith shows up. Faith is knowing and trusting.

There was a time I tried to operate in faith, but wasn't certain what faith really was. I once thought faith is just hanging on until something changes. There are elements of patience in faith, but I have to know what faith is to see the substance and the evidence.

1. Faith, by definition, is "conviction of the truth of anything." That is the meaning of the Greek word translated *faith* in the New Testament. Or, we can say that faith is being convinced that something is true.

Since faith is the conviction that something is true, it logically follows that until you are convinced that something is true, you are not in faith.

2. Faith is the substance. That word substance means "a setting under, a thing put under, a substructure, a foundation."

EVERY DAY IS A FAITH DAY

If we believe something is true, we have a foundation. We have something firmly established under us when we are convinced that a thing is true. Until then, we have no foundation. We have nothing to stand on as we move from one point to another. We have nothing to build on or to rest on until we are convinced something is the truth.

Faith is the evidence of things not seen. We can insert the word "yet" into that sentence. Faith is the evidence of things not seen yet.

3. Evidence means "proof or that by which a thing is proved or tested."

The conviction that something is true gives me a foundation, something on which to rest. My conviction that something is true is proof that I believe. I know I have faith in my heart when I am convinced something is true. Until that conviction shows up, until I am convinced, there is no faith. I can have knowledge of Scripture. I can know what the Word of God says, but I must possess a conviction that it is the truth.

JOHN 17:17

17 Sanctify them through thy truth: thy word is truth.

From time to time, I put my left hand on this Scripture and raise my right hand to God and say, "I choose from this day forward to believe every word in this book as absolute truth. It is truth in the absolute sense. I am convinced of that. That is my conviction. The Word of God is true."

It is not a truth. It is *the* truth. Jesus said, "*...I am the way, the truth, and the life...*" (John 14:6). The Word of God is not just a truth; it is the truth. If the Word of God

FAITH IS A "STANDING ON"

is just "a truth" to us (just one of many truths), it will be impossible for faith to show up in our lives. We have to be convinced that what the Word of God says is truth!

Our friends, coworkers, and neighbors can doubt and speculate, but it won't change anything of which you are firmly convinced. Circumstances can pressure you to change what you believe, but when you are convinced that the Word of God is truth, then faith has arrived. Faith is the victory that overcomes the world.

PSALM 119:142
142 Thy righteousness is an everlasting righteousness, and thy law is the truth.

The word *law* refers to God's teaching instrument, His Word. God's Word is not one of many truths. It is THE TRUTH.

PSALM 19:9
9 The fear of the Lord is clean, enduring for ever: the judgments of the Lord are true and righteous altogether.

When you are convinced the Word of God is truth, then you are in faith, and you will have a foundation, a substructure upon which you can build. Many people are not convinced that the foundation they are building on is truth. It may sound like a good idea. But until you are absolutely convinced, it is not faith.

God does not mind questions when you ask about something you don't know. When the angel Gabriel came to Mary, he told her that she was going to have a Son and that she was going to name Him Jesus.

19

EVERY DAY IS A FAITH DAY

> **LUKE 1:34-35**
>
> **34 Then said Mary unto the angel, How shall this be, seeing I know not a man?**
>
> **35 And the angel answered and said unto her, The Holy Ghost shall come upon thee, and the power of the Highest shall overshadow thee: therefore also that holy thing which shall be born of thee shall be called the Son of God.**

Mary said, *"...be it unto me according to thy word..."* (Luke 1:38). At that moment, she became convinced. God did not hold it against her because she had a question as to "how" something was going to happen.

But some questions could be evidence of doubt or indicate a lack of conviction. For example, I prayed for a young man to be healed who said, "I know that the Word of God says by Jesus' stripes we were healed, but how can I expect to believe I am healed with all this pain in my body?" I had to help him find a place of assurance so he could receive.

One woman who had been delivered from a life of drug addiction was in the process of rebuilding her life. She asked, "It is hard to believe my needs are met when I have so many things still due. How can I believe?" Those questions are produced by a lack of conviction and will hinder us from receiving by faith.

When you are convinced that your needs are met according to His riches in glory, then lack is not an issue. You have a foundation born of your conviction that your needs will be met according to His riches in glory (Phil. 4:19). You have proof. You have evidence. You have faith

FAITH IS A "STANDING ON"

in your heart, and it is the conviction that something is true. Once you are convinced something is true, there are no more questions.

Notice that Mary never again questioned Gabriel. She didn't say, "I don't know how this is going to happen. I know what the angel said, but I don't know how this is going to happen." When the angel came to Mary, it was the Word of the Lord coming to her.

She didn't have a Bible that contained His words as we have. Mary couldn't read the story and see how it was going to turn out. She had to operate by faith. She had to be convinced that what the angel said to her was the truth. It became the foundation for her to become pregnant with the Son of God and to become the mother of Jesus Christ.

When you are convinced that His Word is truth, faith comes. On the other hand, if you are not convinced the Word of God is truth, then faith hasn't come.

God, Who Cannot Lie

TITUS 1:2
2 In hope of eternal life, which God, that cannot lie, promised before the world began;

One translation says, "*...God, Who cannot deceive...*" Knowing that God cannot lie is essential to the working of faith. The Bible says God cannot lie or deceive.

I want to caution you that some translations say something different about this verse. For instance, one version says, "*...God, Who never lies.*" Another says,

EVERY DAY IS A FAITH DAY

"God, Who does not lie." Both of those translations could undermine your faith.

If I say, "Well, God never lies," it leaves the impression that He can lie, but He never does. How can I be convinced or convicted that what He said is true if there is the possibility that He will lie?

When I was growing up, we used to sing a song that said, "He's never failed me yet." YET? Do you expect Him to fail you? Are you convinced He never will? If you are, don't put the "yet" in there. God has never failed me PERIOD, and He will never fail me. God said that He will never leave you or forsake you (Heb. 13:5).

When someone says, "God does not lie," that still carries the implication that He can lie. God and His Word are TRUTH. They are not a truth; they are truth personified. The truth came from God. God, who is truth, cannot utter a lie. You must be convinced of this. The Word of God is truth. You must take it as a composite whole. The Word of God is truth from cover to cover.

Becoming Convinced in Every Area

When Michelle and I were married, we believed God is a Healer. That was just commonplace for us. But the area of finances was a challenge for us! We were not convinced about God's provision in that area.

We struggled financially for the first few years of our marriage. Something needed to change! I was working all the hours, including overtime, that my employer would

FAITH IS A "STANDING ON"

provide. Michelle was babysitting children and taking as many children as she could. We had kids in our house from early morning until late evening. If I had an opportunity to work on Saturday, I took it. However, we were still coming up short.

The situation improved somewhat when we began to tithe consistently. Yet, we were still not convinced. I was praying and asking God to meet our needs. I was hoping things would change. But I had not yet entered the place of being convinced that what I saw in the Word of God was true.

Here's part of the problem: I didn't have a lot of understanding about what God said about the issue of finances. I didn't know enough truth to establish a conviction.

We made a decision. We said, "We are coming out of this." For 40 days, we turned off the T.V. and all other forms of entertainment (i.e., radio, videos, games, etc.). We didn't listen to anything except the Word of God concerning finances. Also, during my lunch hour at work, I read Kenneth Copeland's book, *The Laws of Prosperity*.

I remember the night I became convinced. I was listening to Dr. Leroy Thompson preach, and all of the Scriptures I had been studying and meditating exploded in my spirit. I shouted with Dr. Thompson at the top of my voice, "I'll never be broke another day in my life!" That was the spark that lit the fuse of my being convinced that God would meet every one of my needs. I was convinced that when I gave, it would come back to me, that God wanted

23

EVERY DAY IS A FAITH DAY

me to have abundance in everything, and that God has already given me richly all things to enjoy. My faith, the conviction of those things, remains unshakeable.

I no longer think, "Somehow, the Lord is going to bring us out." That is not faith. That is religion. I am convinced that I am prosperous. I am convinced that God is the total Source of my supply. I became convinced of that when I believed it was the truth.

What has God told you, either in His Word or through your spirit? What has God told you? Maintain your confidence that it is going to come to pass. The Word you maintain in your possession is the Word that comes to pass in your life. If you don't hold onto it, it won't come into manifestation.

If you ask me, "How do you know you are going to have it?" I am convinced that what God said is true, so I have the proof I need. That is why I don't need to feel better to say I am better. I have the Word of God, and I am convinced.

How Can You Become Convinced?

The proof is not in feeling better or having all the symptoms disappear. The evidence is not when the doctor says I have a clean bill of health. The proof showed up when I became convinced. The promise has to be bigger than the problem. The symptoms will leave, but even before they leave, you must be convinced. We can't believe for something if we have no proof—no faith. We can't accurately believe for something without being convinced.

FAITH IS A "STANDING ON"

ROMANS 10:17

17 So then faith cometh by hearing, and hearing by the word of God.

The conviction that something is true comes by hearing the Word. The conviction that God will meet every one of your needs comes by hearing what the Word says about it. Being convinced you are healed of the Lord and that your body is whole and strong comes by hearing the Word. The Word of God is truth, authored by God, Who cannot lie.

Faith is a Standing On

Years ago, the Lord gave me a statement. He said, "Faith is not a hanging on; faith is a standing on." He revealed to me that faith is the substructure. Faith is the foundation. Faith is the substance upon which you stand and not something that leaves you hanging on in desperation.

How many times have you heard the statement, "Well, I am just hanging in there." We are not supposed to be hanging in there; we are supposed to be standing.

Or maybe you have heard, "Well, I am just waiting on the Lord." That statement is evidence that we are not convinced! We are not waiting on God because His work was finished from the foundation of the world. We have to be convinced of what He has spoken. Then, faith has come.

"Well, Pastor, I believe that. I just want to see it."

If we have the proof in the Word of God, what else do we need to see? If we are convinced God shall supply all

25

EVERY DAY IS A FAITH DAY

our needs according to His riches in glory, what else do we need to see? That is the proof.

Remember the definitions of these terms:

- Faith is the conviction something is true.
- Substance is the substructure, the foundation, something to stand on.
- Evidence is proof.

I am convinced that God said, "I will supply all of your needs according to My riches in glory." I have a foundation and a substructure under me. I may not see it in the natural, but I have the proof.

I must invest time and attention to being convinced. When I become convinced, it is just a matter of time.

When Abraham was convinced (Chapter 4 of Romans), he started giving glory to God for something he couldn't see yet. But how do we know Abraham became convinced? He started calling things that be not as though they were.

"Calling things that be not as though they were" is not a magic formula. It only works if you are convinced. Why are you calling things that be not as though they were? It is because you are convinced that what "isn't" really "is."

CHAPTER THREE

Unchangeable

Jesus Christ the same yesterday, and today, and forever.
—Hebrews 13:8

JESUS IS TODAY WHAT HE WAS yesterday, last year, and 2000 years ago. And He will be the same forever because His character never changes.

How can I be sure it is God's will to heal everybody every time? Well, you can look back 2000 years ago at the ministry of Jesus Christ and find that He never failed to heal anybody who came to Him. He never said, "It is not My will to heal you."

There were times when multitudes of people came to Jesus. The Bible says He taught them the Word of God and healed all their sick. There were times He looked out over the crowd, had compassion on the multitude, and healed them all!

EVERY DAY IS A FAITH DAY

Jesus is good. He is our Forgiver, Healer, and elder Brother. Jesus wants the best for us. He is the same today as He was when He ministered to people. We can have faith in our future because Jesus will be the same forever.

It is dangerous to be more convinced of an experience than what the Word of God says. Natural circumstances do not change God's Word or hold more influence than what God has spoken. Our conviction has to be based upon the written Word of God, which Jesus Himself declared to be truth.

When I see it in the Word, I believe it. God can't lie, and Jesus is the same yesterday, today, and forever. This stability provides the substructure for our faith.

God never changes, and His faith never changes. Faith comes the same way it has always come (Rom. 10:17). Faith grows the same way it has always grown and operates the same way it has always operated. While each person may have a different measure of faith, it will function the same.

HEBREWS 6:17-18

17 Wherein God, willing more abundantly to shew unto the heirs of promise the immutability of his counsel, confirmed it by an oath:

18 That by two immutable things, in which it was impossible for God to lie, we might have a strong consolation, who have fled for refuge to lay hold upon the hope set before us:

The word *immutability* refers to the unchangeableness of God's counsel. The counsel is God's promise, which

UNCHANGEABLE

He confirmed by an oath. We can identify aspects of this promise in the following verses:

GENESIS 12:1-3

1 Now the Lord had said unto Abram, Get thee out of thy country, and from thy kindred, and from thy father's house, unto a land that I will shew thee:

2 And I will make of thee a great nation, and I will bless thee, and make thy name great; and thou shalt be a blessing:

3 And I will bless them that bless thee, and curse him that curseth thee: and in thee shall all families of the earth be blessed.

✳✳✳

GENESIS 17:1

1 And when Abram was ninety years old and nine, the Lord appeared to Abram, and said unto him, I am the Almighty God; walk before me, and be thou perfect.

✳✳✳

GENESIS 15:1-2

1 Fear not, Abram: I am thy shield, and thy exceeding great reward.

2 And Abram said, Lord God, what wilt thou give me, seeing I go childless, and the steward of my house is this Eliezer of Damascus?

Abraham was not initially convinced of the things that God had spoken to him. So, to confirm His promise, God told Abraham to get a ram, a she goat, and a heifer. Abraham split all three of them down the middle and

EVERY DAY IS A FAITH DAY

laid them one right after the other. God made a binding covenant, or blood oath, with Abraham by walking through those pieces. The complete account of God's covenant with Abraham is recorded in Genesis 15:9-18.

God Will Do What He Promised

He swore a blood oath to Abraham, and this is the same oath that is sworn to us also. The Bible says this oath is unchangeable.

HEBREWS 6:18
18 That by two immutable things, in which it was impossible for God to lie, we might have a strong consolation, who have fled for refuge to lay hold upon the hope set before us:

God cannot lie. We have His promise and His blood-sworn oath as a foundation for our faith, along with a strong consolation that God won't change His mind!

Faith is more than just not paying attention to what you see. I knew a woman who said she was in faith about her bills, but she just kept putting them under the rug! She didn't even open the envelope. When their electricity eventually got turned off, her husband said, "I thought you paid the bills."

She said, "I've been in faith." Evidently, she had not; the lights were turned off!

Faith doesn't hide things or deny things. Faith confronts the situation fully convinced that God supplies all your needs.

UNCHANGEABLE

2 CORINTHIANS 4:13

13 We having the same spirit of faith, according as it is written, I believed, and therefore have I spoken; we also believe, and therefore speak;

Many people try to convince themselves by making faith declarations, but that is not what this verse is saying. Your faith is designed to be drawn out of the heart by your words. When you say, "By His stripes I am healed," you say it because you are convinced it is true. We believe and speak our faith.

Looking Past the Seen

2 CORINTHIANS 4:18

18 While we look not at the things which are seen, but at the things which are not seen: for the things which are seen are temporal; but the things which are not seen are eternal.

You can be convinced of something that has a greater reality than the present state of your situation. This gives you the ability to look past what is seen and focus on the unseen, without denying your present circumstances. You can look past the symptoms and see yourself healed. You can look past the financial need and see yourself out of debt. You can look past the behavior of your loved one and see them born again. How do you get there? You become convinced.

When the doctor says, "This is how it is going to be," something rises up in you and declares, "I don't believe it is going to be that way. I say it is going to be this way." You are not denying what exists. It is there. But you don't

EVERY DAY IS A FAITH DAY

accept it as the final verdict, nor do you allow yourself to be convinced it is the truth. God's Word is truth.

How do you look at what is not seen? The simple one-word answer that people give is, "Faith!" While that is correct, we need to remember our definition of the term *faith*. When we read the Scripture, "...*For we walk by faith and not by sight...*" (2 Cor. 5:7), we apply our definition to read, "We walk by what we are convinced of, and not by what we see."

The battle is taking place to prevent us from being convinced of God's Word. The circumstance will try to convince you that it is the truth. You must choose the one of which you are convinced. You have to acknowledge, "I choose to believe God." When you make a choice to be convinced by the Word of God, faith comes, and you have proof.

Abraham's Faith

No one can determine how much faith someone has by looking at them. No one can measure who has big faith, medium faith, or small faith. But everybody can develop the faith that will change their circumstances. Faith is personal.

> **ROMANS 4:16-17**
> **16 Therefore it is of faith, that it might be by grace; to the end the promise might be sure to all the seed; not to that only which is of the law, but to that also which is of the faith of Abraham; who is the father of us all,**

UNCHANGEABLE

17 (As it is written, I have made thee a father of many nations,) before him whom he believed, even God, who quickeneth the dead, and calleth those things which be not as though they were.

Abraham believed what God said. He was convinced. The Bible shows us how we know Abraham was convinced. He hoped against hope. Hope provides a picture.

ROMANS 4:18
18 Who against hope believed in hope, that he might become the father of many nations, according to that which was spoken, So shall thy seed be.

The first word translated *hope* in this verse means "a constant dread or a constant picture of something bad." The second word translated *hope* means "a picture of good, an expectation of good."

Abraham, from a human perspective, had only a picture or an expectation of a bad outcome. His situation was utterly impossible. When God asked Abraham to come out of Ur of the Chaldees, Sarai was barren (Gen. 11:29-30). She was unable to have children from the day they were married. It was humanly impossible.

This is the inner image Abraham had to overcome. Perhaps Abraham thought to himself, *It has always been this way. She has never been able to have children. Even when I was able to have children, she was barren* (Gen. 11:29-30). Abraham had a picture, but he had to hope against it. He had to become convinced of what God said by focusing on "...so shall your seed be."

EVERY DAY IS A FAITH DAY

ROMANS 4:19

19 And being not weak in faith, he considered not his own body now dead, when he was about a hundred years old, neither yet the deadness of Sarah's womb:

Abraham didn't pay attention to his own body. He knew his condition and Sarah's condition, but these things were not a reason that God couldn't do what He promised. Abraham took what God said as truth, even when faced with the facts. Abraham was faced with all of the details, and yet he did not stagger.

ROMANS 4:20

20 He staggered not at the promise of God through unbelief; but was strong in faith, giving glory to God;

Abraham did not waver or change his mind. He didn't say, "Boy, that is too rough!" Instead, he was strong in faith, giving glory to God.

ROMANS 4:20 AMPC

20 No unbelief or distrust made him waver (doubtingly question) concerning the promise of God, but he grew strong and was empowered by faith as he gave praise and glory to God,

Abraham grew strong as he gave praise and glory to God! If you are in faith, you will be rejoicing.

Abraham Was Convinced!

Your praise, your worship, and giving glory to God is one of the highest expressions of your faith. You need to shout and dance because you are in faith about what God said. You glorify God because you are convinced that God is going to do what He said He would do!

> **ROMANS 4:21**
>
> **21 And being fully persuaded that, what he had promised, he was able also to perform.**

Remember, God is going to lead you by steps. He won't put you out there and expect you to take some big leap. He will lead you to take steps.

I've been in situations where God has talked to me, and I was convinced that when I entered my time of prayer, He would give me my answer. Instead, I prayed and received no further instruction. I could have stayed on the carpet, praying in other tongues until I couldn't talk, but He had already told me what to do. The instruction He had already given was enough, and He was waiting for me to act on it.

Faith Is Not a Grind.

Hebrews 4:3 says they that have believed have entered into rest. Have you done what God told you to do? If you have, then rest. Faith will provide the certainty that will help you avoid worry and maintain peace.

The flesh may compel you to try to do something that seems spiritual, like praying harder or longer to make things work. But faith is enough! The Word of God says, *"Abraham believed God."* Abraham entered into rest. He couldn't change his circumstance in his natural ability, but Abraham became convinced God could and would.

EVERY DAY IS A FAITH DAY

At some point, you must rest. Don't entertain the question, "When will it happen?" *When* is irrelevant. *When* shows up quicker as you rest. The more you try to move it along, the more you will delay your answer.

It is happening! The Word is working right now. If you could heal yourself, you would. If you could change your finances, you would. It is going to take a greater ability than you possess, and faith is the only way that you can tap into this greater ability.

CHAPTER FOUR

Substance and Evidence

FAITH IS BEING CONVINCED that something is true, a surety. Faith comes by hearing the Word of God. Once you are confident that the Word is absolute truth, it gives substance to the things for which you are hoping (Heb. 11:1).

Faith provides a foundation, something on which to stand. The term *substance* carries the idea of a bridge that allows you to travel from one point to another. Faith is the substance and the evidence.

Evidence means "proof or the thing by which something is proven." Once you are convinced that the Word is true, you have something on which to stand; you now have proof because you have faith. When you are convinced that something is true, faith has come. It is a surety.

EVERY DAY IS A FAITH DAY

Faith is not a feeling or a series of events. Faith is not about a car, a house, or a suit of clothes. Faith is a conviction, a surety that what God said is going to come to pass in your life. Once you are convinced, faith has come, and you have a foundation.

We can be convinced in the spirit, regardless of what is seen. Many people think faith is just not looking at what is seen in their natural situation. But the reason we don't look at what is seen is that we are convinced in the heart. You can be confident because you are not seeing the natural only. You are seeing in the spirit.

Faith is not "hanging on." Faith is assurance. No one who is in faith ever ties a knot and just hangs on! Faith is solid; it provides something on which to stand.

Faith isn't difficult because it is the natural response of your recreated human spirit. In the beginning, it may seem different because you had been walking by sight and feelings. You spoke out of your emotions or said what the situation told you. Now you are saying what the Word of God says, despite what the situation says. It is absolutely 100% natural to the born-again believer to live and walk by faith.

Faith is the substance and currency of the kingdom. Faith is the exchange point that is required to do business in the system of God. He designed faith as the means to access His provision.

38

SUBSTANCE AND EVIDENCE

2 CORINTHIANS 4:18

18 While we look not at the things which are seen, but at the things which are not seen: for the things which are seen are temporal; but the things which are not seen are eternal.

Faith is not a denial of the current situation. If we have sickness attacking our body, we don't deny it. There is no faith value in saying, "I don't have anything wrong. I'm not sick."

Instead, we can draw out the currency of faith that has been treasured up in our hearts. If we have deposited Isaiah 35:4-5 in our hearts, we can withdraw the faith it has produced and use it to access the healing that rightfully belongs to us.

ISAIAH 53:4-5

4 Surely he hath borne our griefs, and carried our sorrows: yet we did esteem him stricken, smitten of God, and afflicted.

5 But he was wounded for our transgressions, he was bruised for our iniquities: the chastisement of our peace was upon him; and with his stripes we are healed.

Jesus bore your sickness and carried your diseases, and with His stripes, you are healed. If He bore your sickness and your diseases, then you are healed because He carried your sickness. If it was yours, He carried it.

The Bible never instructs us to walk in faith by not looking at what is seen. Faith sees. Faith sees the eternal established Word. The things that are seen by natural senses are temporal, which can be defined as "temporary and subject to change."

39

EVERY DAY IS A FAITH DAY

We shouldn't allow things that are temporary to move us out of faith. Focusing on the temporary condition of the situation will allow it to gain momentum as it keeps our attention. Instead, we shift our focus to what is not seen.

How do you look at what is not seen? You can focus on what is "not seen" by looking at the Word of God. What does the Word say? You may not see the evidence of it in your body, but you see the evidence of it in the Word. You have the proof because you have the Word of God, and once you have seen it in the Word, the natural circumstances don't hold the same power to influence you.

The things that can be seen are based on natural sense-knowledge evidence, and that is what influences the natural man. The things that are not seen are founded on spiritual, heart-faith knowledge and motivate the spiritual person. The unseen things are eternal, never diminishing in power, strength, or value because they are established in God's Word.

When we think it is hard not to look at what is seen, it is because we have been consistently giving attention to it. If we consistently give attention to the Word of God, the Word becomes more real. We don't need to know every detail in advance. We just need to know what God said about the circumstance.

Keep walking it out because the circumstance will change. Keep "flying by the instruments." You might look at your spiritual radar and see nothing but storms, but there is an end to the storms. What you are dealing with

SUBSTANCE AND EVIDENCE

has an expiration date! Stay with the proof you have found in God's Word.

2 CORINTHIANS 1:9-10

9 But we had the sentence of death in ourselves, that we should not trust in ourselves, but in God which raiseth the dead:

10 Who delivered us from so great a death, and doth deliver: in whom we trust that he will yet deliver us;

Faith that sees beyond the circumstance knows that God did deliver, does deliver, and will deliver. If God ever delivered you in the past, remember that God hasn't changed, and His Word hasn't changed. If God delivered you ten years ago, He will deliver you this year. If He delivers you this year, He will deliver you next year. Keep your faith in what God said!

By the Hearing of Faith

ROMANS 10:17

17 So then faith cometh by hearing, and hearing by the word of God.

The word translated *hearing* in this verse refers to the organ of hearing, the ear. The Bible tells us very simply how faith comes—through what you hear. The Bible-prescribed way for faith to get into your heart is through your ears.

GALATIANS 3:2

2 This only would I learn of you, Received ye the Spirit by the works of the law, or by the hearing of faith?

EVERY DAY IS A FAITH DAY

How do you hear faith? You first hear the Word of God and faith comes as a result. Paul asked the people whether they had received the Spirit by working for it or by hearing the Word about it. We received by hearing the Word about it.

GALATIANS 3:5
5 He therefore that ministereth to you the Spirit, and worketh miracles among you, doeth he it by the works of the law, or by the hearing of faith?

The Galatians were getting into the works of the law and Judaism, and Paul had to warn them. He reminded them they had heard the Word, and it had produced faith. But they were moving away from faith and into works.

When you are moved by what you see, you have entered into works. When you are basing your life on the Word of God, faith is in operation granting legal spiritual access to the thing for which you are believing. You have a right to receive it because you believed it.

ROMANS 4:3
3 For what saith the scripture? Abraham believed God, and it was counted unto him for righteousness.

The Eyes of Faith

In December of 1998, the Lord said to me, "The last day on your job is February 22nd, 1999." It was as plain to me as my own voice. I know it wasn't audible, but it was just as real as if I had heard it with my ears.

42

SUBSTANCE AND EVIDENCE

In line with God's instruction, I made arrangements to step off the job at the insurance company which had been the primary income for my family. February 22nd, 1999, was my last day. Please understand, I didn't anticipate that I was stepping away "from" something. I was convinced that I was stepping "into" something.

But it looked like the situation I was stepping into was not capable of supporting my family. The Lord assured me, "Your family will never want. Nothing will go unpaid. Everything will be covered." Sure enough, it was. The Lord opened the opportunity to enter into full time ministry, and we have continued to experience the provision of the Lord.

But this step of faith did not randomly occur. For the year previous, the Lord had me focused on First Corinthians 9:14:

1 CORINTHIANS 9:14
14 Even so hath the Lord ordained that they which preach the gospel should live of the gospel.

I wrote this verse onto a piece of yellow legal pad paper and put it on the wall of our basement where I studied. Over that year, it became imprinted in my spirit. The Lord prepared us for this step. I had been seeking Him through fasting and prayer. My wife, Michelle, and I had been immersing ourselves in the Word. This was not a blind leap. The faith to make that change was being developed for months before the Lord directed me to move off that job. I was able to take the step with confidence!

EVERY DAY IS A FAITH DAY

The Lord was able to ask me to step off my job and step into pastoring full time because I had spent a year becoming convinced that "they who preach the gospel should live of the gospel." I was convinced of that promise. When the conviction was in my spirit, faith came! It was the most natural thing in the world to step off that job. There was no trepidation, no hesitation. I had heard from God and had invested the time becoming convinced.

Yes, there are times when God will ask you to make a change. There are times God will ask you to step away from something. When it is done in faith, it won't be a step into darkness. You will see what you are moving into with the eye of faith.

There is no such thing as "blind faith." Real Bible faith is never blind. We can see through the eye of faith. We may be "blind" in the sense that we cannot see the whole picture of what God is leading us into, but faith is not blind. Faith is how we can see.

When we step out in faith, we have a direction, a leading. God has given us enough direction to get us started. In other words, we know where we are headed, even though we may not be able to see how it will all play out. Yet, the faith that motivates us to step out is far from blind. As a matter of fact, it is only through faith that you will ever see what God has called you to do. Faith is the bridge that gets you from one point to the other.

What is "walking by faith"? Often, we are conditioned to think that walking by faith is ignoring what we see. Actually, when we walk by faith, we allow faith to be our sight and to guide us. We are not merely refusing to pay attention to what exists. We are focused on a source of information that is of greater stability and truth.

We must do our part, which includes considering what God says to be more real than the current situation. We must believe what God said in His Word more than we believe what we are seeing or feeling.

Walking by faith is not a denial of what presently exists. Many people paint faith as a denial. Remember, the base definition of faith is "being convinced that something is true." That conviction that something is true produces substance and provides something upon which we can stand. Our conviction that the Word of God is true gives us a foundation, a sub-structure.

There is no substitute for spending time becoming convinced that the Word of God is true. My faith was the proof that I wasn't going to fail. It was my conviction, my faith. To have proof is not being able to see it in the natural. To have proof is being convinced of it in the spirit. How do you know things will change? You have the Word of God.

The Word of God Is the Key

God's Word is the basis of faith. What does the Word say? Paul used this phrase over and over: "What sayeth the Scripture?"

Abraham didn't have a Bible, but God spoke to him face-to-face. Abraham believed what God said.

EVERY DAY IS A FAITH DAY

The Bible is God speaking to us. Every time I get a new Bible, I write on the front page, "This is my Bible. This is God speaking to me." In front of Genesis, Chapter One, I write the words, "Dear Philip." At the end of Revelation 22, I write the words, "Love Jesus." It is Jesus' personal letter to me. My Bible is God speaking to me. The Bible is not just a book about somebody; it is Somebody. God's Word is a living entity.

When God speaks to you, it is through faith and through His Word. The same faith God used to speak everything into existence is the faith that you and I possess. We can change anything in our lives through the Word of God.

Abraham believed God. Insert your name into this statement: _____ believes God. Somebody will ask, "How did they get that new house?" They believed God. How did she get healed of that disease? She believed God.

How will you get what you need? You are going to believe God. The way Abraham believed God was putting his faith in the promise! The same promise was made to those who are righteous by faith.

ROMANS 4:13-16

13 For the promise, that he should be the heir of the world, was not to Abraham, or to his seed, through the law, but through the righteousness of faith.

14 For if they which are of the law be heirs, faith is made void, and the promise made of none effect:

15 Because the law worketh wrath: for where no law is, there is no transgression.

16 Therefore it is of faith, that it might be by grace; to the

SUBSTANCE AND EVIDENCE

end the promise might be sure to all the seed; not to that only which is of the law, but to that also which is of the faith of Abraham; who is the father of us all,

The promise says, "I will bless you and make your name great. In blessing, I will bless you, and you will be a blessing. I will protect you and shield you. I will keep you." The promise is sure to all who are heirs of the promise by faith in Jesus Christ.

Never submit to sickness or yield to poverty. Never give in to failure! Choose to believe these things will never triumph over you. Choose to stand, convinced of the Word of God. Choose to be convinced by the substance and evidence provided by God's Word. Mary chose to be convinced and declared, *"Be it unto me according to Your word"* (Luke 1:38).

Choose to believe it and say it. Your faith is the substance of the promise and the proof that you have it.

CHAPTER FIVE

God's Faith Won't Fail

GOD'S FAITH NEVER FAILS! Often, when people say they are standing on the Word of God, standing in faith, but they fail to receive, they call it a "faith failure." Faith never fails, and there are three very important reasons for this:

Reason #1 Faith Comes from God's Word

Faith comes from and is based on the Word of God. Faith for the promises of God (i.e., healing, finances, victory, etc.) comes from the Word of God.

ROMANS 10:17

17 So then faith cometh by hearing, and hearing by the word of God.

EVERY DAY IS A FAITH DAY

Since the Word of God never fails, the faith that the Word produces never fails. Although we may know someone who didn't get the miracle for which they were believing, we can't place the blame on the Word of God. The faith that comes from the Word of God never fails because it is produced by the Word. The Bible lets us know that the Word is unchanging. It cannot change.

Reason #2 It is God's Faith

The faith we have is God's faith. Mark 11:22 says, "And Jesus answering saith unto them, Have faith in God."

Many center-column references say, "Have the faith of God." *Young's Literal Translation* says, *"Have faith of God."* The faith that we possess is God's faith and originates from His Word.

Nothing of God ever fails. For instance, the love that you have is the love of God. According to Romans 5:5, it has been shed abroad in your heart by the Holy Ghost. First Corinthians 13:13 says, *"And now abideth faith, hope, charity* [love]*, these three; but the greatest of these is charity* [love]*."* Verse 8 says that love never fails.

Love never fails because it is God's love. It comes from God. Why does your faith never fail? It is of God!

The believer is a very important component in the proper operation of faith. Our correct participation will determine how faith operates in our lives. When we apply our faith according to the Word of God, our faith will always work. If we misapply the perfect faith of God, and our prayers are not answered, it wasn't the faith that failed.

We have to say these things because people hear teaching about faith and think they can declare something multiple times, and their prayer will be answered within three days. It probably won't be because there are many other elements to the process of faith that are missing.

Jesus didn't teach that if we say something one time or multiple times, it would happen. In Luke 17:6, He said, *"And the Lord said, If ye had faith as a grain of mustard seed, ye might say unto this sycamine tree, Be thou plucked up by the root, and be thou planted in the sea; and it should obey you."*

Some say, "But the fig tree died in one night for Jesus." Jesus, however, was highly developed in believing that He would receive whatever He said. He was skilled in the operation of faith. We can follow His example and become skilled in faith!

Reason #3 God Gave Us This Faith

The faith we have was given to us by God.

ROMANS 12:3

3 For I say, through the grace given unto me, to every man that is among you, not to think of himself more highly than he ought to think; but to think soberly, according as God hath dealt to every man the measure of faith.

God doesn't have two different kinds of faith. He doesn't have a generic, watered-down version for us to use and a

EVERY DAY IS A FAITH DAY

high-potency, name-brand version that He keeps for His use. It is all "God's faith," and He has given to each of us a measure of faith. The measure we received was personally given to us by God. God will not give us something that is faulty.

So, if faith cannot fail, why have some people failed in their faith?

Failure to Rightly Divide the Word of God

2 TIMOTHY 2:15
15 Study to shew thyself approved unto God, a workman that needeth not to be ashamed, rightly dividing the word of truth.

The phrase *rightly dividing* means "to cut straight the Word of God or to cut it right." We must rightly divide the Word of God.

MARK 11:23-24
23 For verily I say unto you, That whosoever shall say unto this mountain, Be thou removed, and be thou cast into the sea; and shall not doubt in his heart, but shall believe that those things which he saith shall come to pass; he shall have whatsoever he saith.

24 Therefore I say unto you, What things soever ye desire, when ye pray, believe that ye receive them, and ye shall have them.

Let's rightly divide the Word found in this text. Jesus said we would have whatever we say. This is important because our words have to line up with the things we say we believe. We have to make the "mouth-heart connection."

GOD'S FAITH WON'T FAIL

We can't say just "anything." We cannot say we are in faith for victory and yet talk defeat. If we do, then we are not in faith.

Faith is a seed that we plant or dig up by our words. To find out what kind of seed we have sown, we look in our garden. If I come to your house and there are watermelons all over your back yard, don't tell me you planted turnip seeds! I will disagree.

You can't say you are in faith for prosperity if you are talking about the problem. I mean, you can say it, but you won't be in faith if you do.

Words Will Strengthen or Weaken Faith

ROMANS 4:20

20 He staggered not at the promise of God through unbelief; but was strong in faith, giving glory to God;

Abraham gave thanks, praise, and glory to God for bringing to pass the promise that he would have a child through which he would become the father of many nations. He didn't see his body changing naturally. He wasn't any stronger physically. Sarah was no more capable of bearing a child at that time than she had been years before.

What did Abraham do? He kept his mouth in line with what God had spoken and continued to call those things that be not as though they were. He was strong in faith, giving glory to God.

You may be dealing with a circumstance, but your faith gets stronger the more you talk to the circumstance,

EVERY DAY IS A FAITH DAY

saying what God said about it. The key to receiving what you say is that you must "be saying it."

The more you declare the Word of God into your situation, the more you will glorify God. Your faith is being strengthened at the expense of your circumstances. Sadly, there are many people who strengthen their circumstances at the expense of their faith!

The more you talk faith, the less strength your circumstance will have. The more you say what God said, the less strength your problem has. You are depleting it of its energy source: the words you say.

If you do not empower the circumstance with your words, it has no power. Your faith needs to hear your words.

"Yes, but my mind…"

You need to vocally speak to your mind because you cannot outthink the thoughts that come to your mind. The adversary can throw a hundred thoughts an hour into your mind. You can't use thoughts to cast down a thought. Instead, you have to open your mouth and declare how it is going to be.

The dominion God delegated to Adam was the dominion of words. When the thought comes that you are not going to make it, open your mouth and say, "No, no, no! Thanks be unto God who always gives me the victory. Thanks be unto God who always causes me to triumph (2 Cor. 2:14). No weapon formed against me will prosper (Isa. 54:17)!"

GOD'S FAITH WON'T FAIL

How many times must you say this? Who is counting? Say it until your faith gets big enough to run those thoughts out of your life.

Words Can Destroy Your Desires

What many people thought was a failure of their faith was actually their words working against them. The words we say can cancel out or destroy the result we desire from the Lord.

MARK 11:24

24 Therefore I say unto you, What things soever ye desire, when ye pray, believe that ye receive them, and ye shall have them.

The integral component is "what you desire." The desired result is the image you have obtained from the Word of God. You say, "I see myself healed." You look in the mirror and say, "I am well and whole in Jesus' name." These are things we should be saying out of the deposit of faith we are treasuring in our hearts.

But many people start out saying, "I am believing God is going to heal me." Then, they use the same power of words to destroy their desired results. "I believe God healed me, but why don't I feel better?"

Wait a minute! The Bible says unbelief hindered the children of Israel from receiving from God because the Word preached was not mixed with faith (Heb. 4:2).

Your tongue is the mixer that will combine your faith with God's Word. You put it in your heart and mix it with

EVERY DAY IS A FAITH DAY

your words. You can unite faith to your circumstances with your mouth. Words can produce life in the circumstance, or they can destroy your crop of healing or prosperity or victory.

Don't destroy your desired results with your words. Nothing will kill the crop of victory in your life quicker than your words. Your circumstances are designed to respond to what you say.

The more you say, "I am healed," the more you starve sickness of the power to make you sick. The more you say, "I am prosperous," the more you starve poverty from the ability to make you poor.

Instead of allowing the problem to overwhelm you, you can end up overwhelming the problem, regardless of the severity of your situation. You have the power of the Word of God backing you.

CHAPTER SIX

A Balance in Believing

WHEN THERE IS A FAILURE IN the application of faith, we know it is not the Word of God that has failed to perform. We know God cannot lie, and we know He is faithful.

If I have missed it, I want to know to avoid the same result again. If what I am doing isn't working, trying harder is not going to fix it. I will just continue in the wrong direction.

Faith doesn't fail. We can fail in the application of faith, the dynamics of faith, the stand of faith, etc. But when faith is applied according to God's Word, it won't fail to do what God designed it to accomplish.

EVERY DAY IS A FAITH DAY

However, many people, attempting to act in faith during a difficult situation, will mistakenly take the wrong action to resolve the situation. That's because their faith is not sufficiently developed. Often, they think the corresponding action will prove they have faith or force God to respond with the answer.

If someone comes to me and says, "I am battling this pain in my body. My heart is racing, and I am short of breath. Do I need to go to the doctor and get it checked out? "

My response is, "YES! Just as fast as you can." The fact that they are asking means they need to go. Yes! The refusal to see a doctor does not prove they have faith. It is not a faith act, and it won't access healing for them.

If you have pain in your body, you can deny it all you want, but you have pain in your body. Denying the pain or the symptoms is not the application of faith, and it will hurt your faith because you will be operating in presumption and foolishness instead of faith.

You may ask, "What if it is nothing?" Then you will know it is nothing. People have died while thinking they were in faith when they could've gone to the doctor and had the problem fixed.

A woman told me, "The doctor said I have high sugar, but I am not receiving that report." Faith would not "receive" it as the final report, but faith won't ignore what the doctor has found either. I encouraged her to follow the dietary guidelines the doctor provided to control her blood sugar levels while she put her faith to work.

A BALANCE IN BELIEVING

Walking out of the doctor's office saying, "No, I don't! I don't have high sugar" is NOT the application of faith. That is denial! You cannot change what you do not confront. To apply faith, you have to confront the problem with the Word of God.

"But, Pastor, we are not supposed to receive those things." We don't submit to that outcome or give up and accept the diagnosis as "hopeless." But if the doctor says you have a certain condition, the Bible doesn't tell you to deny it. That is a failure to understand the proper corresponding action.

The power is found in "calling those things that be not as though they were." Where there is sickness, I am calling for health. "I know this is what the doctor said. I understand it is a reality in the natural, but I call for what the Word of God says." That would be the proper corresponding action of faith.

I have witnessed much error over the past two decades as I have pastored people in the local church. Many people have misconceptions about faith that cause them to take foolish risks and to suffer needlessly. They endure hardships that they shouldn't experience because of a misunderstanding of corresponding actions.

There must be a balance. We don't want to have people throwing their medicine away or failing to go to the doctor because they think they are in faith.

59

EVERY DAY IS A FAITH DAY

Faith Must Be Nurtured

ROMANS 10:17
17 So then faith cometh by hearing, and hearing by the word of God.

There are no overnight successes in the Bible. God's plan for our lives requires that we grow in our faith. Remember, faith comes by hearing; it grows by use and by speaking it. The more you are hearing, using, and speaking faith, the faster your faith will grow and develop.

Faith for the things of God comes by hearing the Word of God concerning those things. You can't just hear the Word in general terms and expect to have faith for specific things.

Someone may be listening to the Word throughout their day. But, if they need healing in their body, the Word of God that speaks of healing should be what they are ingesting. If they are struggling financially, then the primary thing they need to hear is the Word on finances.

They may need to hear the Word on family or marriage. A Wordless marriage is doomed to fail. A husband can't love his wife like Christ loved the church if he is not in the Word, learning how Christ loved the church. Faith for marriage comes by hearing the Word on marriage.

JAMES 2:14-18
14 What doth it profit, my brethren, though a man say he hath faith, and have not works? can faith save him?

15 If a brother or sister be naked, and destitute of daily food [this is the context],

A BALANCE IN BELIEVING

16 And one of you say unto them, Depart in peace, be ye warmed and filled; notwithstanding ye give them not those things which are needful to the body; what doth it profit?

17 Even so faith, if it hath not works, is dead, being alone.

18 Yea, a man may say, Thou hast faith, and I have works: shew me thy faith without thy works, and I will shew thee my faith by my works.

The *profit* described by the word "it" in verse 14 is the profit of faith. What does faith profit? What is the faith he is discussing? It is the faith that person just exercised for that needy brother to have clothes and food.

For example, in speaking to someone in need, suppose you say, "Depart in peace, brother, and be warm and filled. I have faith that God is going to provide you with clothes and groceries." The Scripture says that your faith is not profiting that person because, in this instance, you are trying to show faith without works.

In contrast, the one who says, "I'll show you my faith by my works. I'll buy him a shirt. I will feed him," has a corresponding action in line with his faith.

Faith is accompanied by action. But the action will be in proportion to the faith you have. Many people suffer needlessly, and they call their suffering faith. Their suffering is not faith; it is foolishness.

What Do You Believe in Your Heart?

"If I was healed, I wouldn't have any pain." No, that is not what the Bible says. You won't find any Scripture in

EVERY DAY IS A FAITH DAY

the Bible that says, "If hands are laid on you, and you are healed, you will have no pain." It says Jesus carried your pain. That means it is His desire to alleviate it. If it were instantaneous, what need would there be for faith?

"I believe my children are well, but they don't look like they are getting any better." Wait a minute! What is the corresponding action in your case? You could start by rejoicing in the Word. "Thank God, my children are following the plan of God for their lives. Oh Father, You are doing a perfect work in my children. Thank You that I trained them up the best I knew how to follow the plan and leading of God for their lives. I thank You that my children are following God's plan for them. Even now, the angels are causing events to be set in motion whereby my children will hear the gospel and turn their lives to Jesus."

You hold fast to what the Word of God says. The appropriate corresponding action is to quote the Word of God. If you stay in faith, you will eventually see all those things change. You can't rush the result by taking extreme action. You are not going to paint God into a corner, and make Him do something.

Don't be deceived into thinking, *Well, I need this bill paid by Friday, so I will just write out the check Wednesday and send it in. God will have to supply the money.* No, He won't! You will hear "Boing, boing, boing!" because that check will bounce.

"Yes, but God said..."

God never said, "Thou shalt write a hot check, and I will pay it."

A BALANCE IN BELIEVING

Get up every day, put the Word in your heart, speak it out of your mouth, and things will begin to change. You must do that every day.

The thought may come, *What are you going to do now? You've done all you know to do.* Here's is the proper corresponding action. Rejoice that it is done. Declare, "I've said it, and I believe I have received it." I've operated my faith and have taken the action I can take. Now, I am going to rejoice."

Hope Paints a Picture

HEBREWS 11:1

1 Now faith is the substance of things hoped for, the evidence of things not seen.

Hope is a picture or a goal-setter. The reason why written goals are so effective is that you can see them. If you say you have goals but they are not written down, you are missing a valuable component. The ability to clearly imagine or picture the desired goal provides a building block for your faith. Hope paints the picture and draws the image in your heart.

The picture of what you are believing has to be precise. The Word of God is the picture that hope is drawing, and faith unites us to it. Most of us didn't have a picture of what we could be until we saw it in God's Word. When we saw the image, we went about the process of building our faith. Our faith united us to the picture. Today, many people are living the picture they saw years ago simply because faith joined them to it.

EVERY DAY IS A FAITH DAY

Hope is a wonderful goal-setter and paints a beautiful picture, but it is not a receiver. Hope is not enough to bring the promise into manifestation. Faith is needed to unite us with the picture we are seeing.

An example of uniting faith with a picture image is referenced in Genesis 13:14-15:

> **GENESIS 13:14-15**
>
> **14 And the LORD said unto Abram, after that Lot was separated from, Lift up now thine eyes, and from the place where thou art northward, and southward, and eastward, and westward:**
>
> **15 For all the land which thou seest, to thee will I give it, and to thy seed for ever.**

Abraham had to look first. He had to see something. When God wanted to show him how many descendants he would have, He said, "Go look at the stars. They will be like the sands of the seashore."

God will bring pictures into your life of what you want to be. You must look at the pictures. Then, you must unite faith with it because faith is the substance, the grounds, the title deed, the assurance of the picture. You must see yourself in the picture.

Many have what they call "faith failures" because they stop looking at the pictures. Don't ever go through the motions of faith just to satisfy someone else, saying faith statements so other people will think you have faith. Speak faith declarations for the purpose of keeping the picture alive in you.

A BALANCE IN BELIEVING

It is possible to fail to receive because of the lack of a clear picture. I see myself as healed, prosperous, and successful. What you see determines what you can have.

In the same manner, I could fail to receive, depending on what I am seeing. If I say, "I thought I was better; I thought I was past this," it would be because my picture changed.

Faith is the substance of the image you have. Hope is the goal-setter. What is the goal? These are things we should know. We have heard them, but we must be consistent in establishing the picture by saying, "This is what the Word says, and this is what I will receive."

Maintain Your Faith

When you begin to declare what you are seeing in the Word of God, you paint that picture on the canvas of your life. "This is what I see!" Abraham could maintain his faith.

ROMANS 4:17-19

17 (As it is written, I have made thee a father of many nations,) before him whom he believed, even God, who quickeneth the dead, and calleth those things which be not as though they were.

18 Who against hope believed in hope, that he might become the father of many nations, according to that which was spoken, So shall thy seed be.

19 And being not weak in faith, he considered not his own body now dead, when he was about an hundred years old, neither yet the deadness of Sarah's womb:

EVERY DAY IS A FAITH DAY

Against hope, Abraham believed in hope. There was a natural human picture and a spiritual, biblical, God-given picture. He had to take the picture God had given him and put it against the picture he could see in the natural.

The Bible says that against hope, Abraham believed in hope, that he could become the father of many nations. Abraham could maintain his faith and hope because he kept his focus on what had been spoken. This was what God had said. He didn't consider any other picture that was provided by the natural circumstance as a reason that God could not do what He promised. So, how can a natural circumstance change what God has said would be?

"The Lord said He was going to save my children. But they are acting worse than they ever have." But what did God say? What is the picture you have? That is the picture you must maintain.

Abraham became fully persuaded by focusing on the picture the Word created and allowing faith to unite him to that picture.

CHAPTER SEVEN

The Development of Faith

ANOTHER COMMON MISTAKE in the application of faith occurs when people try to reap a result when their faith for the promise has not reached a full measure of growth.

> **MARK 4:26-29**
>
> **26 And he said, So is the kingdom of God, as if a man should cast seed into the ground;**
>
> **27 And should sleep, and rise night and day, and the seed should spring and grow up, he knoweth not how.**
>
> **28 For the earth bringeth forth fruit of herself; first the blade, then the ear, after that the full corn in the ear.**
>
> **29 But when the fruit is brought forth, immediately he putteth in the sickle, because the harvest is come.**

Earlier in Chapter Four of the Book of Mark, Jesus taught that the Word of God is the seed planted into the

EVERY DAY IS A FAITH DAY

ground of the heart to produce a harvest. In verse 28, the Lord explained a process of growth when He said, "...first the blade, then the ear, after that the full corn in the ear." The person who is exercising faith in a specific area of their life must be patient to allow the Word to grow and develop the fruit of that promise.

The development of faith is a progression—the blade, the ear, and the full corn. If a person tries to harvest the blade, they will destroy their future. The blade is just the sprout. Faith is beginning to bring forth and produce.

Then, if allowed to continue, the growth will progress to the next stage. There is evidence that fruit is on its way. But it is immature. It is not yet everything you need it to be. The corn stalk hasn't matured enough to have the ear of corn.

Some people thought their faith failed when they tried to reap their harvest before the time. A lack of understanding about the growth and development of faith caused them to attempt to harvest the blade or the ear.

For example, I was praying for the sick during a service in our local church. A woman had heard me teaching on faith, and her heart was stirred. When she came up for prayer, she removed her hearing aid and stomped it on the floor. I was shocked!

Although her faith was growing in the direction of healing, it was not ready for harvesting. She could have continued using her hearing aid while she developed her faith for healing. Instead, she was disappointed and gave

THE DEVELOPMENT OF FAITH

up on receiving healing. She thought faith didn't work. As a result, she stopped growing in the Word.

The Bible says, *"For the earth bringeth forth fruit of herself..."* (Verse 28). The ground of our hearts knows what to do with the promise of God's Word. The reborn spirit of the believer will work to bring what we desire. But we have to guard the growth of the Word in the heart until the harvest of faith arrives.

Levels of Faith

Faith can grow from one level to another. It is possible for our faith to grow exceedingly.

2 THESSALONIANS 1:3

3 We are bound to thank God always for you, brethren, as it is meet, because that your faith groweth exceedingly, and the charity of every one of you all toward each other aboundeth;

Peter stepped out of the boat and walked on water with what Jesus called "little faith" (Matt. 14:31). But Jesus labeled the faith used by the woman of Canaan as "great faith" (Matt. 15:28). Jesus marvelled at the faith of the centurion who only needed to have Jesus speak the Word, saying, *"...I have not found so great faith..."* (Matt. 8:10). So, your faith can grow from the level it is currently operating to another level of effectiveness.

But don't try to operate at a level that you are not developed to operate. If you are exercising faith for a different house, at what level can you believe God?

EVERY DAY IS A FAITH DAY

You may say, "I can believe God for whatever I want." But can you really?

If you are currently living in a one-bedroom apartment, have you sufficiently built your faith to believe for a home costing $375,000 that has four-bedrooms, three and a half baths, and a pool in the backyard? Have you really developed your faith to that level? If you have, apply your faith to receive that house. But if you have not matured to that level of faith, you may need to start with a smaller, less-expensive house.

Now, if your faith has not reached a level of maturity to receive a more expensive home, but you go into debt to purchase it anyway, I can promise you that you will constantly struggle to keep that house. Therefore, it is better to grow your faith to a level of maturity to receive that more expensive house without being under pressure and worrying about how you will keep it.

Let's say, for instance, that a person is paying $800 a month for an apartment or a home, and they want to move to a home that will cost $1700 a month. That is more than double what they are now paying, and they may believe it won't be a big deal. To cover the additional cost, however, they will have to believe for, at least, $900 more each month.

I have witnessed people who got into houses that they called a blessing when, in fact, those houses became a noose around their necks. It became a financial struggle for them to make their mortgage payments.

THE DEVELOPMENT OF FAITH

If you want a bigger, better house, where is your faith? Spend time building your faith for a home. Don't just say, "God is going to give me something," and call that faith.

Faith comes by hearing the Word of God. You must listen to the Word of God about your house. This is true for other specific needs like healing, your marriage, finances, etc. You must hear the Word of God about the things God wants to bring to you.

The Interaction of Faith and Patience

HEBREWS 6:12

12 That ye be not slothful, but followers of them who through faith and patience inherit the promises.

Notice that those who operate in faith and patience will inherit the promises. That is a spiritual law, but what is the key to its operation? Obtaining the results of faith will require patience.

Many times, people jump out and do things when they are not developed in faith. When they fail, the blame is often placed on their faith, but their faith didn't fail. They just didn't include patience.

We laugh at the commercials that tell us, "If you take one pill a day, you won't have to exercise or eat right. The pounds will just melt away." That won't happen. Something has to be done. It takes patience. Every day, you must combine a proper diet with exercise to lose weight. As you patiently do this, you will eventually see a change.

EVERY DAY IS A FAITH DAY

You don't want to be the guy who hasn't worked out for five years. On January 1st, he gets a gym membership and goes to one workout. Then, he is ready to pose in the mirror and see a change. However, nothing has changed!

But let that same person develop discipline and work the principles. He will see a change! It may take three months, six months, or a year. At the end of the year, he will see a different person in the mirror than he saw at the beginning of the year. His faith in what he was doing and his patience to keep doing it will pay off!

God's Will Requires Patience

HEBREWS 10:36
36 For ye have need of patience, that, after ye have done the will of God, ye might receive the promise.

Put your faith in the Word of God and say, "What God said is what will happen in my life." Then, get up every day and patiently act on it. You will see the results.

Don't wait until you are right up against a deadline to start developing faith. If you are battling symptoms in your body, don't wait until they are unmanageable before you get into the Word. Deal with those symptoms now.

Even if you have no indication of sickness in your body, that is the perfect time to quote the healing Word of God. Just like we maintain our vehicles with oil changes and new spark plugs to avoid problems, we can maintain our health to resist sickness. We can avoid difficulties by giving the Word of God sufficient time to work.

THE DEVELOPMENT OF FAITH

Perhaps you think *I believe I will get instantly healed*. However, there is no promise in the Word of God that says you or anyone else will be healed instantaneously. The Bible says, *"They will lay hands on the sick, and they will recover"* (Mark 16:18). The recovery could be instantaneous. But it might take a few months, a few weeks, a few days, a few hours, or a few minutes. Maintain patience while your faith is at work, receiving the promises of God.

The Role of Confession

Confession of God's Word is vital in the development of faith. However, a confession of faith is not an end in itself.

MARK 11:23

23 For verily I say unto you, That whosoever shall say unto this mountain, Be thou removed, and be thou cast into the sea; and shall not doubt in his heart, but shall believe that those things which he saith shall come to pass; he shall have whatsoever he saith.

Jesus said we would have whatever we say. But that is not all He said about the conditions surrounding our saying.

Jesus said we had to:

1. Say

2. Doubt not in our hearts

3. Believe

There are two other necessary ingredients to the operation of faith besides just saying it. If saying it was

EVERY DAY IS A FAITH DAY

the only necessary ingredient, there would be no mention of believing or doubting.

It is possible to say something you don't believe and claim that it is a faith declaration. Also, it is possible to say the right words with doubt in your heart. Neither of these would be a correct application of faith.

Believing What You Say

LUKE 6:45

45 A good man out of the good treasure of his heart bringeth forth that which is good; and an evil man out of the evil treasure of his heart bringeth forth that which is evil: for of the abundance of the heart his mouth speaketh.

ROMANS 10:9-10

9 That if thou shalt confess with thy mouth the Lord Jesus, and shalt believe in thine heart that God hath raised him from the dead, thou shalt be saved.

10 For with the heart man believeth unto righteousness; and with the mouth confession is made unto salvation.

A person may say, "God meets all my needs." But if the next day they say, "We are never going to be able to pay all our bills," they are canceling out their faith. When a person is under pressure, whatever is abundantly in their heart will come out of their mouth.

Jesus said a man speaks from the supply that is abundantly in his heart. Since it is with the heart that we believe, we must make sure it is full of the Word of God. The person who declares God's promise one day and

THE DEVELOPMENT OF FAITH

agrees with the problem the next day will not release faith in their words.

First of all, they are not convinced that everything they say will come to pass, which indicates they don't properly understand the role of confession. Confession is not just saying. It includes believing and not doubting what you say. In Mark 11:23, Jesus said that you must say or speak to the mountain and not doubt in your heart, but believe.

What I believe to receive won't just happen because I say it will happen. The declaration of my mouth should be an overflowing stream of what I believe. In other words, I say it because I believe. This ensures that my words are filled with faith.

The person who says God meets all their needs must stay in agreement with what they have declared. If they believe it, they will maintain their declaration.

What You Say, Let It Stay Said.

JAMES 1:26

26 If any man among you seem to be religious, and bridleth not his tongue, but deceiveth his own heart, this man's religion is vain.

To properly apply faith, I must believe everything I am saying is affecting my life. I must believe that *every* word I say is going to come to pass. That is what will motivate me to bridle my tongue and govern the words I speak.

For the confession of the Word to be effective, it has to be constant and consistent.

EVERY DAY IS A FAITH DAY

JAMES 1:5-8

5 If any of you lack wisdom, let him ask of God, that giveth to all men liberally, and upbraideth not; and it shall be given him.

6 But let him ask in faith, nothing wavering. For he that wavereth is like a wave of the sea driven with the wind and tossed.

7 For let not that man think that he shall receive any thing of the Lord.

8 A double minded man is unstable in all his ways.

JAMES 1:8 AMPC

8 [For being as he is] a man of two minds (hesitating, dubious, irresolute), [he is] unstable and unreliable and uncertain about everything [he thinks, feels, decides].

Many Christians are double-minded with the words they say. As a result, they fail to see manifestations of faith. Whatever you say, let it stay said. Faith comes by hearing the Word, and your heart will receive faith as you hear yourself speak the Word.

What I believe to receive won't just happen because I say it will happen. It will happen because I believe it and speak it. My declaration should be a result of what I believe.

What it Means to "Be in Faith"

It is easy to say, "I am believing God for this. I am in faith for that." That statement is fine if you are *really* in

THE DEVELOPMENT OF FAITH

faith. Knowing the principles of faith and being in faith are two different things. Don't deceive yourself.

JAMES 1:22
22 But be ye doers of the word, and not hearers only, deceiving your own selves.

You can know the principles of driving, and yet never drive a car in your life. You may have watched someone drive. They turned the key, put it in gear, pushed something on the floor, and the car went forward. Those are the basic principles of driving a car. Yet, if you get behind the wheel and have never driven a car, you may hurt somebody.

The confession of faith is an element of operating faith. Knowing the principles of faith won't produce the results of faith. We have to learn how to operate faith. If it is not operated correctly, you can get hurt or hurt other people.

A man called me to talk to me about his situation. I recognized fear in his voice. He was quoting the Word and doing the right thing. I agreed with what he said, "Praise God! I agree with that, but there is a little fear in your voice. We have to attack that fear." The confession of faith was there, but if I had let him get off the phone knowing there was fear in his heart, he would have deceived himself.

Being in faith is not just confessing words that sound positive. Faith begins by believing what you see in the Word. Believing God occurs as you take a stand on God's Word. "This is what the Word says; this is where I make my stand." Upon what part of the Word are you basing your faith? Do you have chapter and verse? There must be something specific that God said that you are believing.

EVERY DAY IS A FAITH DAY

2 TIMOTHY 1:12

12 For the which cause I also suffer these things: nevertheless I am not ashamed: for I know whom I have believed, and am persuaded that he is able to keep that which I have committed unto him against that day.

Paul says that he knows the One he has believed and the One that he trusts. Believing produces persuasion. The sound of persuasion comes from a person who is believing God. In comparison, the sound of hope comes from a person who knows what the Word says, but they are not completely convinced yet.

We need hope because we must add faith to hope. But faith produces the persuasion. In other words, believing is being sure. When you know that you know, then you are in faith.

You need hope because you must add faith to hope. But faith produces the persuasion. Believing is being sure. You are in faith when you know that you know and when you are persuaded and confident.

Be Honest About Your Faith Level

It requires honesty to operate faith. You must be honest about whether or not you are persuaded. I have stepped out before saying I was in faith about things, and I wasn't.

2 CORINTHIANS 13:5

5 Examine yourselves, whether ye be in the faith; prove your own selves.

In its perfect context, this verse is talking about our overall Christian faith. If that aspect of faith can be

THE DEVELOPMENT OF FAITH

examined, then our faith in the promise of God can be examined.

Some people think not taking medicine means they are in faith. Others think they are in faith if they quit their jobs. Neither of these are applications of faith. If you can't believe that God can heal you while you are taking the medicine, how are you going to believe Him for healing with the symptoms raging out of control. If you can't exercise faith for God to meet your needs with a job, how are you ever going to exercise faith for God to meet your needs without a job?

Conviction or certainty can help us identify whether or not we are in faith. The presence of faith will be persuaded of what God has declared. Faith is living dependent on God's Truth.

Not having a job isn't the definition of living by faith. Refusing to see the doctor or choosing not taking medication isn't evidence that a person is in faith about healing. This is a misunderstanding that hurts people.

ROMANS 15:13
13 Now the God of hope fill you with all joy and peace in believing, that ye may abound in hope, through the power of the Holy Ghost.

An examination of our faith should reveal joy and peace. They are faith's companions. If we are worried, fearful, crying, etc., we need to hear the Word until faith comes. When we have peace and joy flowing, we have the right symptoms.

79

EVERY DAY IS A FAITH DAY

ROMANS 4:20 AMPC

20 No unbelief or distrust made him waver (doubting-ly question) concerning the promise of God, but he grew strong and was empowered by faith as he gave praise and glory to God,

Believing and glorifying God go hand-in-hand. If we are believing, we are glorifying God. If we are believing, there is the sound of joy and the note of victory. It is the sound of persuasion.

CHAPTER EIGHT

Retain the Word That Was Heard

AS WE HAVE SEEN, MANY PEOPLE think their faith has failed to produce when it is actually a failure to apply the principles of faith correctly. Let's review the reasons for what people call "faith failures," which we have covered in the previous chapters.

1. Failure to rightly divide the Word.

2. Misunderstanding of the corresponding action.

3. Trying to harvest before the fruit is developed.

The next reason we will discuss is another common mistake. It is a failure to retain the Word that is heard. Situations, hardships, distractions, worry, etc., can drain the faith that we once contained. We may think we are standing in faith with a full supply of the Word in our hearts, only to discover our supply level is empty.

EVERY DAY IS A FAITH DAY

Don't Let It Slip!

HEBREWS 2:1

1 Therefore we ought to give the more earnest heed to the things which we have heard, lest at any time we should let them slip.

The word *slip* means "to slip from the mind, or to carelessly pass, to run out as a leaking vessel." The Scripture instructs us to give the more earnest heed to the things we have heard, lest at any time they slip our minds. Unless we make an intentional effort to hold onto it, these truths will slip our minds, or it can run out like water from a leaking vessel.

This is not necessarily indicating that we forget what the Scripture said. Instead, it is referring to the light and revelation we have received being diminished by the difficult circumstance or the focus on other things.

Jesus taught that the Word of God sown into the heart is like seed planted in the ground (Mark 4:20). There were three types of soil that did not experience any Word results. The seed sown by the wayside did not receive proper attention to provide an understanding. In the Gospel of Matthew, Jesus said, *"When any one heareth the word of the kingdom, and understandeth it not..."* (Matt. 13:19). In this instance, giving earnest heed or attention could have produced the understanding needed for the Word to be received into the heart.

The heat of the circumstance affected the seed sown in the stony ground. Because there was no depth of earth to allow the seed to develop a root system, the harvest of the

RETAIN THE WORD THAT WAS HEARD

Word was destroyed. When the Word is given the proper attention and meditation, the roots can grow in our daily lives. With a solid root system, we can continue to walk in love, forgive, or exercise patience during times of stress of adverse situations.

The third type of unproductive soil also indicates the need for proper attention. The elements referred to as thorns include the cares of this world, the deceitfulness of riches, the lust for other things (Mark 4:19). These thorns choked the Word. If the worry can keep a believer's focus, it will starve them of the victory the Word is designed to bring.

Jesus follows up the teaching about the seed and the soil with an interesting teaching point.

MARK 4:24 AMPC

24 And He said to them, Be careful what you are hearing. The measure [of thought and study] you give [to the truth you hear] will be the measure [of virtue and knowledge] that comes back to you—and more [besides] will be given to you who hear.

We are responsible for the measure of thought and study we give to the truth we hear. If we allow our eyes and ears to be inundated continually with information that goes against God's Word, we sabotage the productivity of God's Word. But if we guard our hearts from the deception and maintain our focus on truth, we will retain the revelation and be able to walk in faith.

We attend church, study, and read the Bible to receive a refilling. There may be some who have been on a long

EVERY DAY IS A FAITH DAY

spiritual "drive" and are running on empty. It may take a few services for them to get full.

We need to keep receiving the Word because we are constantly placing a demand on the Word. Every time we dip down into our spirits to grab hold of the Word to battle a circumstance, we have taken something off the spiritual shelf that must be replaced.

When I was growing up, people used cash or checks as the main form of payment. A friend of mine wanted his mom to buy something for him. His mother said, "Honey, I don't have any money on me."

He responded, "Just write a check." He had no comprehension that money was needed to back up the check. Many believers think they can choose to believe without the spiritual deposit to back up the withdrawals they are trying to make.

When we deposit the Word of God about healing or prosperity, we go out full. But circumstances and situations arise that cause a debit on that supply. We must retain the Word we are hearing.

Being United to the Word of God by Faith

HEBREWS 4:1-2 AMPC

1 Therefore, while the promise of entering His rest still remains and is freely offered today, let us fear, in case any one of you may seem to come short of reaching it or think he has come too late.

2 For indeed we have had the good news [of salvation] preached to us, just as the Israelites also [when the good

RETAIN THE WORD THAT WAS HEARD

news of the Promised Land came to them]; but the message they heard did not benefit them, because it was not united with faith [in God] by those who heard.

Faith is what binds us to the Word. Faith comes to unite us with the Word so that we become inseparable.

If you don't have the Word of God, there is no way for faith to come. Without being united to the Word of God by faith, the Word cannot affect lasting change in our lives. If we don't have faith mixed with the Word of God, we have no assurance, no confidence. We have no title deed to the promise we believe to receive.

The title of my car is what unites me to my car. If I don't have a title, I have nothing saying that the car is mine. The dashboard can be monogrammed with my name. I can have a personalized tag on the back. I can produce a bill of sale. But if I don't have a title, there is no way of proving it is mine. The title is proof the car is mine.

Faith unites us to the promise and is our title deed. Faith is the proof that unites us to healing, prosperity or the salvation of our families.

If we don't feel united, or made one, with that promise, knowing with certainty that the promise belongs to us, there is more faith-building that needs to occur. More hearing of God's Word is required.

We should never step out to believe God for something on "not sure."

"Are you in faith?"

"I think so. I hope so."

EVERY DAY IS A FAITH DAY

You're not. Let's build your faith some more.

The life of faith requires us to keep ourselves consistently united to the promises by faith. In Hebrews 4:2, it says the same Word was ministered to the Israelites, and it did not profit them.

That means some people hear the Word of God, but it does not benefit them. The Scripture tells us it was because they didn't mix it with faith.

The tongue is the mixer. We mix the Word with faith by saying, "This is what the Word says. This is what I believe." In the beginning, there will be times when you don't feel it or see it. Once you are united with the promise by faith, it is just a matter of time until manifestation.

Faith is proof, not feeling. Faith is the title deed. I have never *felt* like I had a title. I have a legal document that proves I am married. I am married, whether I feel like it or not.

Take the Bible's promises with the same assurance. "I am healed. I am blessed. I am free." Why? You are united by faith to those spiritual provisions.

CHAPTER NINE

Adding Self-Control and Patience

THERE ARE SPIRITUAL ADDITIVES that must be in place in order for our faith to function at the highest level. As we mature in faith, these elements are necessary for healthy growth.

2 PETER 1:3-8

3 According as his divine power hath given unto us all things that pertain unto life and godliness, through the knowledge of him that hath called us to glory and virtue:

4 Whereby are given unto us exceeding great and precious promises: that by these ye might be partakers of the divine nature, having escaped the corruption that is in the world through lust.

5 And beside this, giving all diligence, add to your faith virtue; and to virtue knowledge;

EVERY DAY IS A FAITH DAY

6 And to knowledge temperance; and to temperance patience; and to patience godliness;

7 And to godliness brotherly kindness; and to brotherly kindness charity.

8 For if these things be in you, and abound, they make you that ye shall neither be barren nor unfruitful in the knowledge of our Lord Jesus Christ.

To walk in faith effectively, we need to add to our faith. Faith is the victory that overcomes the world (1 John 5:4). Also, you have the ability to quench all fiery darts of the wicked by placing the shield of faith in front of you (Eph. 6:16). We have a responsibility to maintain our faith in a strong spiritual condition.

No matter who says, "This faith stuff doesn't work," that is not what the Bible says! The reason why faith is not working for some believers could be that they have not added the necessary components of love, patience, or self-control.

You can eat a big steak at every meal, but you are not getting all the nutrients you need. You need more than steak. You need vegetables and fruit. Everything you need is not in one food group. Even if your diet is mainly vegetables, everything you need is not present in broccoli. You need carrots, legumes, peppers, apples, and bananas. If you don't eat a variety of these things, your overall health could be negatively affected.

Faith is the mainstay, a spiritual staple. But in order for faith to be strong and to withstand all the fiery darts of

ADDING SELF-CONTROL AND PATIENCE

the wicked, the proper spiritual nutrition must be added to it.

Adding Temperance and Patience

In Second Peter 1:6, we see that temperance and patience are two components that should be added to our faith. *The New English Translation* says, "*...make every effort to add*" them. *The Amplified Bible, Classic Edition* says, "*...employ every effort.*" Adding temperance and patience to our faith must be a priority.

The word *add* simply means "to supply." Our faith needs a supply of self-control and patience. By adding them to our faith, it protects us from being barren, which means to be "idle, making no progress, and going no further." Think about that! Have you ever had a sense of being stuck in neutral? This verse could provide the answer.

Just because I have faith doesn't mean it is working. It may not be accomplishing anything. It may be idle or unproductive because it is lacking the necessary additives.

Just because you are married doesn't mean you have a successful marriage. Lovingkindness and honor have to be present. Certain things must be poured into a marriage in order for it to be a good marriage.

I don't want to go through my Christian life having faith, yet knowing my faith is accomplishing nothing. I don't want to hit the accelerator on my "faith-mobile" and just race the motor because my faith is in neutral. This means that I can hit the accelerator until the engine

EVERY DAY IS A FAITH DAY

screams. However, if it is in neutral, my "faith-mobile" won't go anywhere.

Temperance is one of the elements we must add to our faith to put it in gear. *Temperance* means "self-control, the virtue of one who masters his desires and passions." For faith to be at its productive best, self-control must be added. The level of self-control I possess will determine the level at which my faith operates.

A lack of self-control causes faith to be idle and unproductive. This can be seen in a number of areas. It can be an out-of-control temper. It can be unrestrained passions or sinful activity. But it can also be a lack of control over our emotions. Emotions require self-control.

Although we have emotions, we are not supposed to be emotional beings. We are spiritual beings. God gave us emotions to enjoy life, but emotions are not supposed to be our masters. Instead, we use the spiritual tool of self-control to govern our emotions.

The human emotions must be controlled by your born-again spirit. When you are facing a challenge in your life, what is it that tries to get out of control? It is your emotions, and allowing your emotions to remain out of control will stop your faith from working.

Jesus Christ, being our example, was Master of every situation that He encountered when He walked on this Earth. He exercised dominion and control over His emotions, decisions, and passions. You and I can follow His example!

ADDING SELF-CONTROL AND PATIENCE

GALATIANS 5:22-23

22 But the fruit of the Spirit is love, joy, peace, longsuffering, gentleness, goodness, faith,

23 Meekness, temperance...

Temperance or self-control is a fruit of the reborn human spirit that the Holy Spirit produces in our spirit. If you only have a tiny bit of "temperance-fruit" on your branch, perhaps it has not been developed. These spiritual additives need to be developed along with our faith. But we cannot develop faith at the exclusion of these additives. If we do, we will have a large fruit of faith on the branch, but nothing to make it strong.

Some children eat whatever they want during the formative stages of their lives, growing from toddlers to teenagers with no restrictions on what they eat. If the food is junk food loaded with sugar and oil, it can have an adverse impact on their physical growth and vital brain functions.

The same principle can be applied to believers who only feed on teachings and Scriptures that appeal to them. The essential teachings and sermons about forgiveness, submission, or humility are often passed over. As a result, their growth, maturity, and development are stunted.

Make the Choice to Develop

Yielding to any aspect of the fruit of the Spirit is a daily choice we must make. Continually submitting to the flow of the fruit of the Spirit is how we walk in the Spirit.

EVERY DAY IS A FAITH DAY

GALATIANS 5:16
16 This I say then, Walk in the Spirit, and ye shall not fulfil the lust of the flesh.

To develop in temperance we have use it, to put it into action. The definition of the word *temperance* includes the idea of "harnessing the desires and passions." As we choose to walk temperately, we regulate our lives in line with the leading of God's Spirit. We harness our desires and passions by yielding to God's love, joy, patience, and longsuffering that are resident in our born-again spirits. This is how we are going to succeed. We could say:

Weak temperance, weak faith.

Weak faith, weak temperance.

When any part of our flesh is out of control, it will hinder the working of faith. That is not just referring to sinful behavior. It can include frustration or fear. If anger is out of control, it will sabotage our faith.

GALATIANS 5:19
19 Now the works of the flesh are manifest, which are these; Adultery, fornication, uncleanness, lasciviousness,

Lasciviousness means "unbridled excess or lack of restraint." In lasciviousness, there is nothing holding you back. Notice the contrast between the fruit of the Spirit and the works of the flesh. The works of the flesh include a lack of restraint, while the fruit of the Spirit involves temperance or self-control.

Faith works at a higher level in a heart that has developed temperance. For instance, some people want to use their faith to fix their finances, but they refuse to

ADDING SELF-CONTROL AND PATIENCE

establish a budget and follow it. They say, "I know we make more money than this. Why don't we have more money?" They are out of control and spend every dollar they receive. However, they want to make faith declarations to change their situation.

How can they properly apply faith? They don't even know where their money is going. This is a genuine example of how lasciviousness affects daily decisions.

Perhaps you have known people with heart issues related to eating fried or fatty foods. The doctor gives them a strict diet, but they won't stick to it. They want prayer or faith to fix it, but their faith needs self-control to be added to the situation.

The doctor may tell you, "You have to stop eating sweets. You are battling diabetes." But you may desire to stop by the bakery and buy long johns and cupcakes with sprinkles. You need to yield to the spiritual supply of self-control and set aside the desserts and candy! You are trying to develop faith for healing, and need to avoid anything that is hurting your body.

Many major diseases can be reversed or stopped by changing what we eat. But people like what they like and consider that to be a good reason to continue in their destructive behavior. "I like potatoes fried in lard. I'm just going to eat them because the fries at that fast food restaurant are the best."

EVERY DAY IS A FAITH DAY

Temperance Is a Spiritual Fruit that Manifests in Your Natural Life.

I don't have to work my faith nearly as hard as some people because I have done my best to employ temperance. I have disciplined myself not to do those things that harm the body God gave me and then try to use my faith to correct it. That's like reading the "do not ingest" warning on a bottle of drain cleaner and saying, "God said that if I drank any deadly thing it wouldn't hurt me. I confess this won't hurt me." The person then foolishly drinks some of the drain cleaner. The following week, people are attending the person's funeral because what they drank was poison!

Marathon runners have to train and build up their bodies. They must be purposeful with their nutrition because they are in training. If they want to be successful, they must hydrate. They don't eat for pleasure. Instead, they eat for fuel. They are tempering themselves. They know that on a certain date, they will be participating in a 26.2-mile race.

No one is conditioned to run 26.2 miles all the time. It takes an intentional and focused effort. When the marathon begins to post the times of each runner, you will see the letters DNF show up next to some names. It stands for "Did Not Finish." Others may say, "They gave it their best shot." However, that was not their goal. They intended to finish the race.

94

ADDING SELF-CONTROL AND PATIENCE

We are not in this walk of faith to "give it our best shot." We are in this walk of faith to win. To win, we have to finish the race! We are in training to win the gold.

The Spiritual Additive of Patience

Let's reread our text in 2 Peter 1:6:

2 PETER 1:6
6 And to knowledge temperance; and to temperance patience.

The word *patience* means "steadfastness, constancy, cheerful or hopeful endurance." This definition helps us to understand that patience is more than "waiting." The application of patience affects how you wait. The Lord told me years ago, "One of the most important things in your life is this: You must be constant every day, every week, every year." Constancy is required in the faith walk.

Patience is cheerful or hopeful in its steadfastness. Patience does not have a long face. I heard a story about a little boy who had never seen a mule before. He ran out to the barn and peeked in a stall to see a mule standing there with its long face. The boy ran back in the house and said, "Mama! That mule has got the same kind of religion Grandpa's got!"

Patience is not grumpy or sad. Instead, it is cheerful and hopeful. It is not "putting up with something." When we are patient, we are constant. Patience is not just waiting; it is waiting in an attitude of cheerful hope.

EVERY DAY IS A FAITH DAY

Patience is a characteristic of those who won't be turned from their deliberate purpose. We must be determined by saying, "This is what I am going after, and this is what I am going to have. I'm not going to deviate or be distracted from that goal!"

We can't get up tomorrow and allow the circumstances to move us away from our objective. However, many people are derailed because they become impatient and quit. They have not developed the fruit of patience, which enables us to remain steadfast or unchanging in our purpose. Faith doesn't empower you to be steadfast. Patience does!

Our text identifies temperance as the first thing that has to be added to our faith. Next, we add patience. When a person has perfect self-control and is willing to be patient, you have a person who is on their way to God's success.

Some say, "Well, this is what God told us, but nothing seems to be changing." Be patient! I am not just telling you to "hold on." Be patient. Don't allow yourself to be moved or distracted from your goal.

> **HEBREWS 10:35-36**
>
> **35 Cast not away therefore your confidence, which hath great recompense of reward.**
>
> **36 For ye have need of patience, that, after ye have done the will of God, ye might receive the promise.**

After you have done the will of God, employ patience. You have to be cheerfully and hopefully expectant. So, be constant and steadfast after you have done what God has told you to do!

ADDING SELF-CONTROL AND PATIENCE

To say, "Well, I have given, and nothing is working" is not being constant or steadfast. When we tithe and give financial offerings, we put patience to work. We allow God's Word to continue working in our situation. We don't have to see it to believe it is working. Instead, we trust and maintain our expectancy.

I know we have all felt like saying, "I thought surely this difficulty would be over by now." That way of thinking can be a trap because people will struggle in their faith, focused on a time frame. If God told you six months, then you can believe for six months. If God didn't give you a certain time frame, don't impose one on the situation because that will sabotage your patience.

When you have done the will of God, be patient.

Are You Patient and Longsuffering?

"Pastor! I have given my children to the Lord. I believe they are saved, but nothing is changing." Be patient!

Did you declare that not only you, but your household would be saved? Then you and your household will be saved. Don't entertain the question: "But why is it taking so long?" Length of time is not going to hinder the plan of God because God is patient and longsuffering.

2 PETER 3:9 AMPC
9 He is long-suffering (extraordinarily patient) toward you, not desiring that any should perish, but that all should turn to repentance.

EVERY DAY IS A FAITH DAY

You have need of patience so that after you have done the will of God you will obtain the promise. Patience keeps your faith in gear over an extended period of time. You have to stay connected to the promise of God.

HEBREWS 6:11-12

11 And we desire that every one of you do shew the same diligence to the full assurance of hope unto the end:

12 That ye be not slothful, but followers of them who through faith and patience inherit the promises.

The word *followers* mean "imitators." We should imitate those who went before us and who obtained God's promises through faith and patience. Faith with the additive of patience caused them to inherit the things God had promised.

"Why is it taking so long?" is a statement of impatience. On the other hand, patience will cause us to say, "I will believe God, no matter how long it takes. I am not going to be impatient." We will see that as our patience grows, our faith is equipped to continue.

2 PETER 1:8

8 For if these things be in you, and abound, they make you that ye shall neither be barren nor unfruitful in the knowledge of our Lord Jesus Christ.

When you develop and maintain spiritual attitudes of temperance and patience, you will not be unproductive or barren. Faith must have these additives. If you have the determination to be cheerfully and hopefully expectant, steadfast, and constant, you will start to see things change.

ADDING SELF-CONTROL AND PATIENCE

Patience is putting consistent pressure on what God said and having a cheerful and hopeful expectancy that what God said will occur. Patience will prepare us to be ready for what God is bringing to us. We just have to be patient.

The Spiritual Additive of Knowledge

2 PETER 1:5

5 And beside this, giving all diligence, add to your faith virtue; and to virtue knowledge.

This word *knowledge* means "awareness, or intelligent insight." *The New Testament: An Expanded Translation* by Kenneth Wuest calls it *"experiential knowledge."*

Faith will be limited when it lacks knowledge. Often, people have the misconception that faith works best in the dark. They think the less knowledge they have about a situation the better their faith can work.

A lady once approached a minister and said, "Would you agree with me in prayer about something?"

He said, "I will if you tell me what it is."

She said, "Do I have to?"

He answered, "Well, if you don't tell me, how am I going to agree?"

Faith is limited when it lacks knowledge. Knowledge doesn't hinder faith. According to Peter, knowledge adds to our faith.

99

EVERY DAY IS A FAITH DAY

The Knowledge of a Situation Doesn't Hinder Faith

Years ago, I approached a woman in my church who had been struggling with some serious symptoms. I asked if she had been to the doctor to find out what was causing the pain and symptoms. She said, "I don't want to find out what is going on because I don't want to hinder my faith." The knowledge of a situation doesn't hinder our faith. As a matter of fact, knowledge of a situation often enables us to exercise our faith on a higher level. It enables us to focus faith exactly where it needs to be applied.

My wife, Michelle, often teaches against praying a "scatter-load prayer." She is referring to a shotgun shell that releases its contents in a scattered pattern. This shell can't be aimed at a precise point. Instead, it spreads out and makes a minimum impact on a general region. We don't want our faith or prayers lacking the accuracy to impact the situation.

If you are facing a financial difficulty, don't just pray, "Oh, bless me Lord. Prosper me! Meet my needs." That is a generalized prayer that won't make a significant change to the situation. If you know you don't have enough income to meet your basic needs, you can pray for an increase in salary or for overtime opportunities on your job. If you are overspending, you can ask God for wisdom and guidance to spend responsibly.

I was praying for people in the church and invited anyone who need to be healed to come forward for prayer. A certain man came forward and said, "I have something

ADDING SELF-CONTROL AND PATIENCE

wrong in my body." But when I asked if he had been to the doctor, he responded, "No. I don't want to get a bad report. I just want the Lord to heal me." He was avoiding the doctor because he was afraid of the knowledge he might receive. He was in fear of what the doctor might say. In that instance, he was not in faith because fear was directing him.

When the doctor gives us knowledge, it can enable us to properly apply faith. We can aim specific requests, declarations, and faith toward the target. Because of knowledge, we can precisely apply our faith to whatever needs to change.

A great example of this unfolded in the life of a young family who had a new baby boy. The young mother had placed the baby in the baby carrier and placed the carrier on the kitchen table while cooking. A skillet of grease ignited on the stove, and she grabbed it to take the smoking pan toward the open kitchen door. On her way, she slipped, spilling the hot grease directly on her baby boy.

The damage to the child's skin was extensive, and his life was hanging in the balance. The members of the church where they attended began to rally around the family. They provided a force of faith and prayer to help that family turn the situation.

The first thing the parents asked of the doctors was, "What do we need to happen for our baby to live through this?" The medical staff explained that his vitals needed to stabilize before they could even begin to administer

101

EVERY DAY IS A FAITH DAY

the treatment needed. The family, along with the group of praying believers, took their assignment and began to pray.

As the vitals became stable, the treatment plan to treat the burns was the next thing on the agenda. The medical staff did not offer any hope of a normal life for this baby. The doctor reported that the child would never be a father, never play sports, etc. He tried to explain to the parents, "There are no skin buds left for new skin to grow. It is impossible for skin to regrow here. There is not even enough skin left on his body to do a skin graph."

They responded, "I understand what you are saying. But if there were skin buds, his skin could grow back?"

"Yes," the doctor replied, "but all of the skin buds are burned away. He no longer has any."

The prayer team began to pray for skin buds to form, and to the doctor's amazement, the skin buds appeared within a few days. With each medical obstacle, the people of faith made their specific petitions until the child was well and whole. He grew up playing sports and leading a quality life. Praise the Lord!

Knowledge was a key element in the success of their faith. Because they knew what needed to change, they could apply their faith in a way that dominated the situation.

ADDING SELF-CONTROL AND PATIENCE

Faith Is Not Afraid of Your Circumstance

Faith does not have to be "kept in the dark" because faith is not hindered by the knowledge of the circumstance. Bible-faith is based on the established Word of God and is not moved by the ups and downs of the situation.

The balance in the application of faith allows us to be aware of the problem without being obsessed by the problem. We don't have to allow the knowledge of the circumstance to pull us over into human reasoning. At the same time, we are not afraid of knowledge.

> **MARK 9:20-21**
>
> **20 And they brought him unto him: and when he saw him, straightway the spirit tare him; and he fell on the ground, and wallowed foaming.**
>
> **21 And he asked his father, How long is it ago since this came unto him? And he said, Of a child.**

Jesus wasn't asking this question just to make conversation. He was accessing knowledge. Jesus wanted to know how long the boy had been this way.

> **MARK 9:22-23**
>
> **22 And ofttimes it hath cast him into the fire, and into the waters, to destroy him: but if thou canst do any thing, have compassion on us, and help us.**
>
> **23 Jesus said unto him, If thou canst believe, all things are possible to him that believeth.**

The New Testament: An Expanded Translation by Kenneth Wuest says, *"As for these words of yours, 'If you are able' — all things are possible to the one who believes."*

EVERY DAY IS A FAITH DAY

The knowledge of the situation did not hinder the application of Jesus' faith. Why would Jesus ask if it was not important for Him to know? I personally believe it was because Jesus needed to know more about the situation to know how to approach it. While the Bible doesn't tell us exactly why Jesus asked, it does tell us that Jesus asked the boy's father how long his son had been in his condition.

> **MARK 9:24-25**
>
> **24 And straightway the father of the child cried out, and said with tears, Lord, I believe; help thou mine unbelief.**
>
> **25 When Jesus saw that the people came running together, he rebuked the foul spirit, saying unto him, Thou dumb and deaf spirit, I charge thee, come out of him, and enter no more into him.**

You may say, "See there! Jesus knew what He was dealing with. He knew it was a spirit." He may have, but I want you to see something interesting.

> **MARK 9:17**
>
> **17 And one of the multitude answered and said, Master, I have brought unto thee my son, which hath a dumb spirit.**

Jesus was given natural knowledge of the problem. When the boy was thrown down by the spirit, Jesus asked his father how long ago did he become possessed by this spirit.

I am not eliminating the possibility that Jesus could have known this by the revelation of God's Spirit, but unless Jesus was operating in the gift of discerning of spirits, and unless the Holy Spirit gave Him special insight, He was operating as a man in this situation.

104

ADDING SELF-CONTROL AND PATIENCE

Natural Knowledge Did Not Hinder Jesus' Faith

Never forget that Jesus had to use His faith. Things didn't happen for Jesus just because He was Jesus. Jesus had to believe what the Father had said. Jesus had to believe what was said about Him. Jesus used His faith!

What hinders the faith of many is that they are afraid that the knowledge of their circumstance will somehow hurt the application or the working of their faith. It did not hurt the application of Jesus' faith, and it won't hinder the application of your faith.

JOHN 11:1-4

1 Now a certain man was sick, named Lazarus, of Bethany, the town of Mary and her sister Martha.

2 (It was that Mary which anointed the Lord with ointment, and wiped his feet with her hair, whose brother Lazarus was sick.)

3 Therefore his sisters sent unto him, saying, Lord, behold, he whom thou lovest is sick.

4 When Jesus heard that, he said, This sickness is not unto death, but for the glory of God, that the Son of God might be glorified thereby.

This is what stood out to me as I read those verses: They told Jesus that Lazarus was sick, and I realize the argument can be made that Jesus may have already known this. But I am not sure that this argument has a firm footing since the Word does not confirm that Jesus knew. Again, the Word says that they had to tell Jesus that Lazarus was sick.

EVERY DAY IS A FAITH DAY

JOHN 11:4 AMPC

4 When Jesus received the message, He said, This sickness is not to end in death; but [on the contrary] it is to honor God and to promote His glory, that the Son of God may be glorified through (by) it.

Jesus didn't respond by saying, "Oh! That's a bad confession. Don't tell me that!" No. He essentially said, "Okay. He's sick, but the end result will not be death. God will get the glory." The news didn't change His faith. The knowledge didn't change what Jesus believed.

Reasoning Can Hinder Faith

Most of the time, it is not the knowledge we have about a situation that hurts our faith. Instead, it is the natural reasoning that hurts our faith. We can receive news or details about a situation and then contemplate how hard it will be to fix the situation. We can become obsessed with how impossible the situation seems to be. If we mix our natural human reasoning into the problem, it will hurt our faith.

When they told Jesus that Lazarus was sick, Jesus immediately responded in faith. He said that this will not end in death; instead, it will end in God being glorified.

Jesus had knowledge and knew how to pray. He knew how to believe. We have no evidence that Jesus knew Lazarus was sick before He was told.

JOHN 11:34

34 And [Jesus] said, Where have ye laid him? They said unto him, Lord, come and see.

106

ADDING SELF-CONTROL AND PATIENCE

Jesus had to ask where they had buried Lazarus. This Scripture reveals that Jesus needed knowledge. If Jesus was going to raise Lazarus from the dead, He needed to know where he had been buried. That might seem simplistic, but it is a key point. I must be able to combine knowledge with my faith.

> **JOHN 11:40-42**
>
> **40 Jesus saith unto her, Said I not unto thee, that, if thou wouldest believe, thou shouldest see the glory of God?**
>
> **41 Then they took away the stone from the place where the dead was laid. And Jesus lifted up his eyes, and said, Father, I thank thee that thou hast heard me.**
>
> **42 And I knew that thou hearest me always: but because of the people which stand by I said it, that they may believe that thou hast sent me.**

Jesus was not saying, "You've heard Me in the past concerning many different things." Instead, He was essentially saying, "Father, You have heard Me concerning what I am about to deal with. You've heard Me!"

Now, notice that John 11:6 says that even after Jesus learned that Lazarus was sick, He still stayed where He was for two more days. Then, Jesus said they were going to Judea again. By that time, it was established that Lazarus had died. They asked Jesus why they were going, and He replied, *"Our friend Lazarus sleepeth; but I go, that I may awake him out of sleep"* (verse 11). In verse 14, Jesus plainly said, *"Lazarus is dead."* So, Jesus had knowledge that Lazarus was sick. He then received knowledge that Lazarus had died. It still didn't change what Jesus was believing.

107

EVERY DAY IS A FAITH DAY

JOHN 11:43-44

43 And when he thus had spoken, he cried with a loud voice, Lazarus, come forth.

44 And he that was dead came forth, bound hand and foot with graveclothes: and his face was bound about with a napkin. Jesus saith unto them, Loose him, and let him go.

Jesus received the knowledge that Lazarus was sick. He received the knowledge that Lazarus was dead. It does not change the outcome. Faith will not be affected by the knowledge you have of your circumstance unless you get over into human reasoning and begin to reason your way out of what God wants to do for you. This is key.

Faith Does Not Abandon Common Sense

Faith is not abandoning what you know you should do. Faith is being convinced that what God said is true, even in the face of the knowledge you may receive. In the face of the circumstance, I still believe. The Word of God will ultimately determine how things are going to be. That is what Jesus was expressing when He said that this will not end in death, but God will get glory for raising Lazarus up.

MATTHEW 9:18

18 While he spoke these things unto them, behold, there came a certain ruler, and worshipped him, saying, My daughter is even now dead: but come and lay thy hand upon her, and she shall live.

The man says very plainly that his daughter was dead. He gave Jesus this knowledge right away.

108

ADDING SELF-CONTROL AND PATIENCE

MATTHEW 9:23-25

23 And when Jesus came into the ruler's house, and saw the minstrels and the people making a noise,

24 He said unto them, Give place: for the maid is not dead, but sleepeth. And they laughed him to scorn.

25 But when the people were put forth, he went in, and took her by the hand, and the maid arose.

In the Gospel of Matthew, they said that the ruler's daughter was dead. In Mark 5:22 and Luke 8:41, we see that the ruler's name was Jairus, and in contrast to the Gospel of Matthew, the Gospels of Mark and Luke both indicate that the ruler's daughter was about to die. In Mark 5:35, people provided Jairus with additional knowledge when they said, *"...Thy daughter is dead: why troublest thou the Master any further?"*

MARK 5:36 AMPC

36 Overhearing but ignoring what they said, Jesus said to the ruler of the synagogue, Do not be seized with alarm and struck with fear; only keep on believing.

Jesus shows us how to deal with the knowledge of a circumstance. Keep on believing! In other words, what they told Jairus would not change the outcome if Jairus would continue believing.

Don't Fear the Knowledge of Your Circumstance

The Word of God says, *"A thousand shall fall at thy side, and ten thousand at thy right hand; but it shall not*

EVERY DAY IS A FAITH DAY

come nigh thee" (Ps. 91:7). Keep your focus on what God said.

Remember, faith doesn't need to be kept in the dark. Adding knowledge to my faith can enable my faith to work on a greater level.

> **1 JOHN 5:4**
> **4 For whatsoever [or whosoever] is born of God overcometh the world: and this is the victory that overcometh the world, even our faith.**

Faith overcomes regardless of what knowledge you possess or do not possess concerning your situation. Don't be afraid to add to your faith the knowledge of what you are facing. People may try to deal with a situation in faith without adding knowledge, but that is how they get hurt.

You must spend time gaining knowledge of what the Word of God says so your faith can be strong and you can be convinced. When you have natural knowledge of a problem, you will still be able to use your faith to overcome it.

In fact, specific knowledge of the situation or problems allows you to apply your faith more effectively to change that specific problem. In any case, faith overcomes, regardless of what knowledge you have or do not have about the situation.

110

CHAPTER TEN

Adding the Force of Love

CHARITY IS BETTER DEFINED as love. It is specifically referring to the same kind of love that God has for us. Until love is added to my faith, my faith will be weak and ineffective because faith is love dependent.

> **GALATIANS 5:6 AMPC**
> **6 For [if we are] in Christ Jesus, neither circumcision nor uncircumcision counts for anything, but only faith activated and energized and expressed and working through love.**

In *The New Testament: An Expanded Translation* by Kenneth Wuest, Galatians 5:6 says, "But faith coming to full expression through love..."

The Amplified Bible, Classic Edition, says, "For [if we are] in Christ Jesus, neither circumcision nor uncircumcision counts for anything, but only faith

EVERY DAY IS A FAITH DAY

activated and energized and expressed and working through love." Notice these four words to express the integral part that love plays in the operation of faith. It says that faith is *activated*, *energized*, *expressed*, and *works* through love.

Have you ever used an industrial-strength binding compound? For example, if you buy a compound to put a rearview mirror on a windshield, there are two components: an adhesive and an activator of the adhesive. The adhesive is not ready to hold the mirror in place until the activator is added to it. In the same manner, faith is activated by love. Faith is not ready to be applied without love.

Romans 12:3 says that every born-again believer has been given a measure of faith. But that measure is activated as love must be applied.

Once we put faith and love together, we are ready to see things change. There may be a situation that has been slow in changing, but when love abounds, faith will grow. And faith is the victory that overcomes the world (1 John 5:4).

Is Something Missing?

Years ago, my wife decided to make her grandmother's blackberry cobbler recipe. She had the recipe card out on the counter and followed it to the "letter." When the cobbler came out of the oven, it was hot and steaming. My children and I waited expectantly to taste this delicious

ADDING THE FORCE OF LOVE

treat. Michelle spooned a portion onto my plate, and I dug into it. Then, I stopped! She said, "What's wrong?"

I said, "Something is missing."

She took a bite of it and said, "Oh, my! Something is missing." She had forgotten to put sugar in it! We had blackberries. We had a beautiful crust. But what was missing was a vital ingredient that made those tart blackberries sweet.

Many people discover that their faith is not working effectively, and the reason is that they are not walking in love. The Bible says we are to be perfected in love, which means walking in mature love. Maturing in love takes time, emphasis, and focus.

Faith in Proportion to Love

I have encountered people in the gym who only like to work on the muscles in their arms, shoulders, and chest. Every day, they curl weights to work their biceps. Then, they go to a machine to work their triceps. However, they have tiny legs because they never work on their lower body. As a result, their upper body is out of proportion to their lower body.

It is not as much fun to work on the leg muscles, in addition to the fact that they are not considered to be the "glamor muscles." However, if I want my faith to grow in proportion to love, attention must be given to both.

In the same way, if we want to be strong in faith, we have to develop in love. Although maturing in love may

EVERY DAY IS A FAITH DAY

not seem glamorous, it is vital to the working of faith. An overemphasis on developing faith and an under-emphasis on developing love will leave us unbalanced. The aspect of greater importance is that our love grows because love gives us the opportunity to properly exercise faith.

Love can be challenging to develop because we have to deal with other people, confront difficult circumstances, be willing to forgive, and refuse to be offended. All of these things are involved in walking in love.

> **1 CORINTHIANS 13:5 AMPC**
> **5 It is not conceited (arrogant and inflated with pride); it is not rude (unmannerly) and does not act unbecomingly. Love (God's love in us) does not insist on its own rights or its own way, for it is not self-seeking; it is not touchy or fretful or resentful; it takes no account of the evil done to it [it pays no attention to a suffered wrong].**

It will take practice to develop in love to the extent that we do not act unbecomingly, insist on our own rights, or become resentful.

With undeveloped love, you will have sub-par faith. If your love is not developed, your faith will be weakened. Without perfected love in my life, I will never have perfect faith. I will never have strong or mature faith.

Your Faith May Be Lacking Love

> **1 THESSALONIANS 3:10 AMPC**
> **10 [And we] continue to pray especially and with most intense earnestness night and day that we may see you face to face and mend and make good whatever may be imperfect**

ADDING THE FORCE OF LOVE

and lacking in your faith.

The Apostle Paul said there was something lacking in their faith. He desired to see them and help them "make good" whatever was lacking in their faith.

1 THESSALONIANS 3:12-13 AMPC
12 And may the Lord make you to increase and excel and overflow in love for one another and for all people, just as we also do for you,

13 So that He may strengthen and confirm and establish your hearts faultlessly pure and unblamable in holiness in the sight of our God and Father, at the coming of our Lord Jesus Christ (the Messiah) with all His saints (the holy and glorified people of God)! Amen, (so be it)!

Notice the phrase in verse 12 that says, "*...to increase and excel and overflow in love....*" As we increase in love, God is able to strengthen, confirm, and establish our hearts faultlessly pure and without blame in holiness. Undeveloped love will inhibit your ability to walk in a high level of faith and holiness. Accordingly, our obedience to develop in love is the catalyst to an effective faith walk!

Faith Is Love-Dependent

Now, as we begin to mature in love, watch out! Things will start happening because our faith will work at a higher level. In tapping into love, we will access the energy source that causes faith to be effective in our lives.

2 THESSALONIANS 1:3
3 We are bound to thank God always for you, brethren, as it is meet, because that your faith groweth exceedingly,

EVERY DAY IS A FAITH DAY

and the charity of every one of you all toward each other aboundeth;

Exceedingly growing faith and abounding love are inseparable. Faith is love-dependent. If your faith is growing exceedingly, you can be sure your love is abounding.

Full-Grown Love Turns Fear Out the Door

1 JOHN 4:18 (AMPC)
18 There is no fear in love [dread does not exist], but full-grown (complete, perfect) love turns fear out of doors and expels every trace of terror! For fear brings with it the thought of punishment, and [so] he who is afraid has not reached the full maturity of love [is not yet grown into love's complete perfection].

When we walk in love, we will have no fear that things won't turn out well. We won't be tormented with fear of rejection, fear of insufficient finances, fear of death, etc. Love will drive the fear out and faith will be supercharged.

Without perfected love, you will not have perfected faith. Perfected love casts out fear. If you are dealing with a situation and thoughts come to you about bad things that could happen, that is fear. It could mean that you are not sufficiently grounded in the love God has for you. You must know that God loves you so much that He is not going to let you fail. He is going to see you through. It is going to be okay!

People you know who operate their faith on the highest level will also be the people who operate love on the

116

ADDING THE FORCE OF LOVE

highest level. Faith and love are inseparable. Faith has to be applied every day, and our love walk has to be exercised every day.

In a marriage, if a wife has strong faith in her husband, it is because love has been developed. Where love has not been developed, there will be little or no faith in that relationship. When a wife knows how much her husband loves her and when a husband knows how much his wife loves him, there is security in that relationship. It is the same way in the spirit. As such, you could say the following:

No faith, no love.

No love, no faith.

Weak faith, weak love.

Weak love, weak faith.

Love is the Main Spiritual Additive to Faith

JAMES 2:14-18

14 What doth it profit, my brethren, though a man say he hath faith, and have not works? can faith save him?

15 If a brother or sister be naked, and destitute of daily food,

16 And one of you say unto them [making a good confession over them], Depart in peace, be ye warmed and filled; notwithstanding ye give them not those things which are needful to the body; what doth it profit?

17 Even so faith, if it hath not works [of love], is dead, being alone.

EVERY DAY IS A FAITH DAY

18 Yea, a man may say, Thou hast faith, and I have works: shew me thy faith without thy works, and I will shew thee my faith by my works.

"I have faith for you Brother. I am praying for you!" People have made statements such as this when they encounter people in need. The Bible says that if we do nothing to help that person, our faith is dead. Why? It is because faith is activated by love (Gal. 5:6 AMPC).

Understand what James is saying. If a person is not walking in love, the confessions of faith and quoting of Scripture are dead. They are alone. But when we add an expression of love to our faith, we will act. This concept is found in First Corinthians 13:1-2.

1 CORINTHIANS 13:1-2 (AMPC)

1 If I [can] speak in the tongues of men and [even] of angels, but have not love (that reasoning, intentional, spiritual devotion such [a]as is inspired by God's love for and in us), I am only a noisy gong or a clanging cymbal.

2 And if I have prophetic powers (the gift of interpreting the divine will and purpose), and understand all the secret truths and mysteries and possess all knowledge, and if I have [sufficient] faith so that I can remove mountains, but have not love (God's love in me) I am nothing (a useless nobody).

Paul mentions some gifts of the Spirit in these Scriptures, and that they are ineffective without love as the motivation. You may have the working of the word of wisdom or knowledge, or the gift of faith, but without love, those gifts are not going to be effective.

ADDING THE FORCE OF LOVE

So, for instance, I can have so much faith that I could move mountain after mountain, but if I don't have love, it doesn't profit me! That large amount of faith is doing me no good because it is dead. It is not activated by love.

Gifts of the Spirit are best operated through a heart of love. Love is the foundation of the gifts of the Spirit. The evidence of spiritual maturity is not getting a word from God or getting a word of prophecy. It is your ability to walk in love.

Love Never Fails

1 CORINTHIANS 13:8 (AMPC)

8 Love never fails [never fades out or becomes obsolete or comes to an end]. As for prophecy (the gift of interpreting the divine will and purpose), it will be fulfilled and pass away; as for tongues, they will be destroyed and cease; as for knowledge, it will pass away [it will lose its value and be superseded by truth].

The Bible does not say that faith never fails. It says that love never fails. The God-kind-of faith always works, but the additive of love must be at work. When faith and love are coexisting and working together, faith will always work because love never fails.

One of the primary avenues for the use of my faith is love. Peter said we must exercise it. Exercising your love is more than just not being offended. On the contrary, it includes all of the following:

- Exercising love is refusing to be offended.
- Exercising love is having compassion.

EVERY DAY IS A FAITH DAY

- Exercising love is being generous.

- Exercising love is paying no attention to a suffered wrong.

- Exercising love is forgiving.

Love is natural to your reborn human spirit. The Bible says we are born of love. God is love (1 John 4:8). One of the first things Jesus commanded us to do is to love one another. I must yield to the love command. I must desire to grow in love.

1 CORINTHIANS 12:31
31 But covet earnestly the best gifts: and yet shew I unto you a more excellent way.

Remember that in the original letter to the church in Corinth, there were no chapter headings. Paul had just explained the gifts of the Spirit. Paul said he would show them a better way, and he started talking about love. All of the gifts of the Spirit are important, but the better way is love.

Follow After Love

1 CORINTHIANS 14:1
1 Follow after charity, and desire spiritual gifts, but rather that ye may prophesy.

Notice that the verse does not say, "Follow after spiritual gifts, and desire charity." Instead we should follow after love and desire to operate these gifts.

I've seen many pastors who could preach very well. At first, I couldn't understand why their ministries were

ADDING THE FORCE OF LOVE

faltering. When I began to interact with them more closely, it became clear. They weren't walking in love.

Walking in love will compel you to forgive people. It is not your responsibility to determine whether they deserve forgiveness or not. Our job is to act in faith and forgive. We want our love to keep step with our faith.

Let's examine what Jesus taught about faith in Chapter 11 of the Book of Mark.

MARK 11:22-26

22 And Jesus answering saith unto them, Have faith in God.

23 For verily I say unto you, That whosoever shall say unto this mountain, Be thou removed, and be thou cast into the sea; and shall not doubt in his heart, but shall believe that those things which he saith shall come to pass; he shall have whatsoever he saith.

24 Therefore I say unto you, What things soever ye desire, when ye pray, believe that ye receive them, and ye shall have them.

25 And when ye stand praying, forgive, if ye have ought against any: that your Father also which is in heaven may forgive you your trespasses.

26 But if ye do not forgive, neither will your Father which is in heaven forgive your trespasses.

It is interesting that verse 25 begins with *"and."* It is connected to the previous three verses. Many people try to speak to the mountain with the expectation that the mountain will eventually move, but their obedience to verse 25 is lacking.

EVERY DAY IS A FAITH DAY

It is imperative that we forgive and become well developed in love. Love activates faith. It is the energy source for faith.

We don't want to be offended or carry a grudge! If those things are operating in our lives, there is no faith operating. Without faith, we cannot accomplish what God wants us to do.

The Lord said this to me years ago, "You are too hard! There are places I won't be able to take you because of it."

Although my motive was to get people to do the right thing, I was not walking in love. I had to change. I had to learn to season my actions and my words with love.

Love in the Marriage Affects the Faith for the Home

I PETER 3:7

7 Likewise, ye husbands, dwell with them according to knowledge, giving honor unto the wife, as unto the weaker vessel, and as being heirs together of the grace of life; that your prayers be not hindered.

Without honor between the husband and wife, their prayers would be hindered. We could identify a lack of honor in the marriage as being a violation of the love command. Love honors the other person.

In a marriage relationship, honor is vital. My wife and I exhibited an attitude of honor for each other in front of our children. We didn't raise our voices or use harsh words.

ADDING THE FORCE OF LOVE

The phrase *as unto the weaker vessel* doesn't mean that wives are weaker spiritually or below par in some way. Peter says to honor your wife as someone who should be cared for, as someone of great value. If husbands don't act on this value, their prayers will be hindered. In this instance, we see a great example of how faith can be hindered by a lack of love.

While this example points to the marriage relationship, it is true in all relationships. If we are not walking in love, if there are disagreements and strife, our prayers will be hindered. We must be governed by love.

As a pastor, I don't want to stand before people who need to get an answer and not have it because I failed to walk in love.

Now, some say, "We need to pray and fast more. If you want power, you need to fast." However, there is not one Scripture in the Bible that says people will get more power if they fast. Not one!

It is a good thing to fast, but the Bible doesn't say it will increase your power. Rather, the Bible says walking in love will increase power in your life. Our faith is energized by God's love at work in us. Faith operates and functions through love.

We Will Never Go Wrong Walking in Love

Do you seem to come up against the same wall time after time? Are you walking in love? Before you make a decision about something, go in with an attitude of love.

EVERY DAY IS A FAITH DAY

Don't hold grudges, unforgiveness, or bitterness against anyone.

Make a decision to walk in love, and you will see your faith work on a greater level. Be willing to correct or forsake some things. You can walk in a greater level of love!

CHAPTER ELEVEN

Daily Faith for Daily Victory

MARK 11:22 WUEST
22 And answering, Jesus says to them, Be constantly having faith in God.

This is the basis for our concept that *Every Day is a Faith Day*. As believers, we should be using our faith for something every day. Faith is not merely a subject to be studied. Faith is our lifestyle (Rom. 1:17).

When Jesus spoke to the fig tree in Mark 11:14, the tree began to die immediately. The next day, the results were very evident as it was *"...dried up from the roots"* (Mark 11:20). Jesus was not capable of doing this by means of an exclusive type of "Jesus-faith." No! Jesus was operating in the same faith that every believer has. It comes from hearing the Word of God (Rom. 10:17).

EVERY DAY IS A FAITH DAY

During the time of His ministry on Earth, Jesus constantly used His faith, which was full of potency. For Jesus, every day was a faith day. When He spoke to the tree, His faith-filled words went directly to the root system of that tree and caused them to wither.

You can choose to use your faith every day and develop the potential of your ability to believe. You can maintain the condition of your heart so that your words will be filled with faith. As a result, your words will carry your faith into the situation and effect change.

Learn to Be Specific

MARK 11:23

23 For verily I say unto you, That whosoever shall say unto this mountain, be thou removed, and be thou cast into the sea; and shall not doubt in his heart, but shall believe that those things which he saith shall come to pass; he shall have whatsoever he saith.

Faith does not work with generalities. Faith works with specifics. Jesus said we must "say" to the mountain.

We are to specifically give the situation a command. If you do not speak specifically to your mountain, it will just hang around. Accordingly, to move your mountain, you need to open your mouth and say, "I speak to you, mountain of adversity. I command you to cease to exist. Be completely removed from my life, never again to return."

After you tell your mountain what to do, begin to dance and rejoice knowing that Jesus said you would have what

126

DAILY FAITH FOR DAILY VICTORY

you say! Get ready to see the mountain move and never return.

Faith Is Voice Activated

2 CORINTHIANS 4:13

13 We having the same spirit of faith, according as it is written, I believed, and therefore have I spoken; we also believe, and therefore speak;

The Apostle Paul is quoting from Psalm 116:10, directly connecting the actions of believing and speaking to the spirit of faith. If I am operating in faith, I am going to be speaking. According to the Word of God, if I am not speaking, I am not completing the process of faith.

Because we believe, we speak. If we believe we are healed, we will say that we are healed. If we believe we are prosperous, we will say that we are prosperous. This is how we activate our faith.

The faith that we have in our hearts must be released. Our words release our faith into the situation. Then, faith brings into the seen realm the promise that was previously unseen to the natural eye and mind.

Here is a very simple explanation. When you call the pizza place and order a pizza, you tell them with your words exactly what you want. You cannot see the person to whom you are speaking. You cannot see the ingredients they are going to use to make your pizza. Yet, you believe that what you said you wanted is what you are going to receive. So, when the pizza is delivered, it does not surprise

127

EVERY DAY IS A FAITH DAY

you that you received what you ordered because it is what you said you wanted.

It is the same way with faith. When you say, you are ordering what you want. Faith, being the obedient servant of the believer, goes to work to produce and bring to you what you desired.

Faith is Founded on the Word

MATTHEW 8:5-10

5 And when Jesus was entered into Capernaum, there came unto him a centurion, beseeching him,

6 And saying, Lord, my servant lieth at home sick of the palsy, grievously tormented.

7 And Jesus saith unto him, I will come and heal him.

8 The centurion answered and said, Lord, I am not worthy that thou shouldest come under my roof: but speak the word only, and my servant shall be healed.

9 For I am a man under authority, having soldiers under me: and I say to this man, Go, and he goeth; and to another, Come, and he cometh; and to my servant, Do this, and he doeth it.

10 When Jesus heard it, he marvelled, and said to them that followed, Verily I say unto you, I have not found so great faith, no, not in Israel.

Jesus told the centurion that He would come to heal his servant. For many people, the fact that Jesus would come to their house to heal their servant would have been preferred. But this man told Jesus to *"...speak the*

128

DAILY FAITH FOR DAILY VICTORY

word only, and my servant shall be healed." Accordingly, following is a summary of verses 5 through 10:

1. The greatest faith involves the speaking of God's Word.

2. The greatest faith is becoming Word-of-God minded.

3. The greatest faith is confidence in God's Word and its authority alone. The centurion had confidence in the Word of Jesus to heal his servant.

4. Confidence in God's Word always brings results. God honors His Word. The centurion's servant was healed and made whole.

Jesus called this display of faith "the greatest faith." Based on our text, this expression of faith needs no additional evidence other than the Word. When we make the decision that we need no other evidence than what the Word of God says concerning whatever we may be facing, we can operate what Jesus called "the greatest faith." We can develop our confidence in God's Word and the authority of God's Word over our circumstances. This is the key to developing effective daily faith.

Faith Gives Us Constant Victory

Since every day is a faith day, we would be scriptural to declare that every day is a victory day.

1 JOHN 5:4
4 For whatsoever is born of God overcometh the world: and this is the victory that overcometh the world, even our faith.

EVERY DAY IS A FAITH DAY

1 JOHN 5:4 WUEST
4 Everything that has been born of God is constantly coming off victorious over the world. And this is the victory that has come off victorious over the world, our faith.

We do not have to pursue victory. When we were born again, we obtained the victory that Jesus won for us in His death, burial, and resurrection.

The Apostle John said "whatsoever" or "whoever" is born of God overcomes the world. *The New Testament: An Expanded Translation* by Kenneth Wuest lets us know that whoever is born of God is *"constantly coming off victorious over the world."*

The world he is speaking of is not this planet. The Bible is referring to the world's system that is under the control of our enemy, Satan.

However, the emphasis of 1 John 5:4 is not on Satan or the world's system. His emphasis is on our victory and the system we operate.

Years ago, I worked for a large insurance company. Now, within this company, there were regular postings for job openings in different departments. Also, each job announcement disclosed the minimum requirements applicants had to meet to qualify for each position. And it just so happened that most of these job announcements stated that the applicant had to be proficient in using the company's computer operating system.

In the kingdom of God, our operating system is the FAITH operating system. Faith in what Jesus Christ has accomplished always causes us to be victorious. The faith

DAILY FAITH FOR DAILY VICTORY

system is a closed system. It cannot be hacked by the devil because he cannot understand faith.

You and I not only have faith, we are of faith. Faith was given to us at the new birth and is part of who we are as believers. As we stay in the Word, our faith grows and grows. We see victory after victory after victory.

Every day is a victory day because my faith always causes me to stand in victory.

A Prayer for Salvation and Baptism in the Holy Spirit

Heavenly Father, I come to You in the Name of Jesus. Your Word says, "Whosoever shall call on the name of the Lord shall be saved" (Acts 2:21). I am calling on You. I pray and ask Jesus to come into my heart and be Lord over my life according to Romans 10:9-10: "If thou shalt confess with thy mouth the Lord Jesus, and shalt believe in thine heart that God has raised him from the dead, thou shalt be saved. For with the heart man believeth unto righteousness; and with the mouth confession is made unto salvation." I do that now. I confess that Jesus is Lord, and I believe in my heart that God raised Him from the dead.

I am now reborn! I am a Christian—a child of Almighty God! I am saved! You also said in Your Word, "If ye then being evil, know how to give good gifts unto your children: HOW MUCH MORE shall your heavenly Father give the Holy Spirit to them that ask him?" (Luke 11:13). I'm also asking You to fill me with the Holy Spirit. Holy Spirit, rise up within me as I praise God. I fully expect to speak with other tongues as You give me the utterance (Acts 2:4). In Jesus' Name. Amen.

About the Author

Pastor Philip Steele is the founder and Senior Pastor of Faith Builders International, as well as the President of Faith Builders International Fellowship. Pastor Steele's desire is to impart faith and hope into the lives of people so that they can overcome any situation. He is dedicated to seeing people and families succeed.

Known for his practical teaching style, Pastor Steele ministers the Word of God through intense, relevant, faith-building sermons. He and his wife, Pastor Michelle Steele, made the decision to devote their lives to ministry by preaching in churches, prisons, juvenile detention centers, and on the streets.

Pastor Steele is devoted to raise up and train leaders to serve in the local church. He considers the following Scripture to be a mandate in his life: "And the things that you have heard of me among many witnesses, the same commit to faithful men, who shall be able to teach others also" (2 Timothy 2:2).

Through the Faith Builders International Ministerial Academy, Minister's Etiquette, and Father's Circle, Pastor Steele pours into the lives of leaders to prepare them for their service in the ministry.

Books by Pastor Philip Steele

Every Day Is a Faith Day

Fear-Free Living

First Words Matter/Last Words Stand

Refusing the Care

The Local Church: The Hope of the World

(All titles available in Spanish)

Books by Pastor Michelle Steele

Finding God's Answers

Intervention Prayers

Maintaining Our Joy

Now You See Me...Now You Don't!

Pressure? No Problem! Expanded Edition

Redeemed and Righteous by Nature

The Guilt, the Shame, and the Blood

The Peace that Comes from Being Made Whole

Walking in the Graveyard

(All titles available in Spanish)

For More Information

Faith Builders International Church

8390 Peoria St/ PO Box 452

De Soto, KS 66018

Office: 913-583-1670

Faith Builders Church of Little Rock

10500 West Markham Ste. 110

Little Rock, AR 72205

Ministry Mailing Address

Faith Builders

PO Box 242692

Little Rock, AR 72223

www.buildfaith.net